MW00637044

Libby Appel

Mask Characterization

An Acting Process

Southern Illinois University Press

Carbondale and Edwardsville

Copyright © 1982 by the Board of Trustees,
Southern Illinois University

Printed in the United States of America

Edited by Teresa White

Designed by Richard Hendel

Production supervised by Kathleen Giencke

Photographs by Phillip Beck

Library of Congress Cataloging in Publication Data

Appel, Libby, 1937–
    Mask characterization.

    Includes index.
    1. Acting.   2. Masks.   I. Title.
PN2071.M37A6   792'.028   81-9157
ISBN 0-8093-1039-2 (pbk.)

To Jessica, Annabel, Madelyn,

Turkey, Naomi, Jake, Madeline,

and Amelia, and the many other Masks

I have met and loved—

and to Estelle Spector,

my dear friend and colleague

Contents

Illustrations

Foreword

This is a wonderful book. It offers what I believe is an inspired suggestion: that the mask, the oldest of the devices we mortals have created to confront the unknowns in our universe, be used as a part of the actor training process.

To the extent that the actor accomplishes that most difficult of tasks, to become someone else, enormous physical and psychic demands are made on his/her creative spirit.

The mask, older than theater, older most likely than the surviving forms of religion, is a potent instrument for transformation and understanding.

Libby Appel in this book offers teachers of acting a detailed view of a way of working with masks. While the underlying assumptions are profound, the reader will find a wealth of practicality and specificity.

Acting, one of the almost unteachable subjects, can be learned with the help of a good teacher. Teaching can be advanced with the help of a good text. This is one which should be of practical and inspirational use to teacher and learner alike.

John Ransford Watts
Dean
Goodman School of Drama,
DePaul University

Preface

The creative process is something of a mystery. The artistic product is the result of trial and error. It begins with something as vague as intuition, which might then be coupled with the recollection of personal history. What follows is an intellectual process where these sensory and imaginary "data" are defined, refined, shaped, and enlarged until the artist is satisfied with the result.

Actors, as creative artists and skilled craftsmen, must reach the deepest core of this personal experience in the creation of their roles. It is this experience which forms the roots of the creative process. It is only after this groundwork has been prepared that the intellectual selection and justification of acting choices can take place. It is not uncommon for an actor to respond to stimuli in set behavioral patterns. Consciously or unconsciously, he has placed boundaries on his imagination, and the result shows in his work. When faced with the creation of a character outside his immediate source of experience, the actor's body may remain stiff and ungiving, his behavioral choices trite, stereotyped, or simply dull. This repetition of old patterns results in "personality acting" or just plain bad work.

In order to prevent this atrophy of the imagination, a process is needed which will integrate the actor's skills with his instincts, allowing impulses and imagination to flow in conjunction with a flexible and vulnerable body. It needs to be a process which will release and open the actor's emotional and physical range so that he can bring renewed inspiration to his work on a script.

In response to this need, the mask characterization process was developed into a technique class for actors through the combined efforts of Estelle Spector, head of movement training at the Goodman School of Drama, and myself. Although the use of the mask in actor training is not unusual, Ms. Spector and I utilize it for a very specific purpose. Not only do we wish the actor to experience the established results of working with masks—that of stimulating the imagination, putting greater emphasis on physical actions, acting with the whole body, and ridding the actor of self-conscious mannerisms—but we want the actor to create a complete, fully dimensional character which could be re-created after the mask had been removed—a character which has little or no relationship to the actor's social persona. Sixteen weeks of concentrated work are employed to discover, develop, and expand this character.

Because of the tremendous safety behind the mask, the use of it impels the actor to create such a character. The masked actor represents someone other than himself, and this anonymity produces a miraculous sensation of freedom. With the mask acting as a "permission-giver," the actor can do anything, be anyone. He can plumb deep into his resources and tap his soul, imagination, and experiences. By covering, the actor uncovers.

The mask, then, becomes the perfect tool for the actor. It allows the freedom to dare to be someone else, and at the same time to be more himself. It forces the actor to organize his body to communicate a thought. It frees the imagination to permit new experiences. It becomes safe to communicate with absolute commitment and flexibility. When the body and the imagination are exercised and enriched, the actor develops a sense of confidence in his ability to create. Confidence in the process of creation is fundamental to the artistic product, and the mask characterization technique encourages such development.

Unlike other acting classes or rehearsal situations, in mask characterization the actor works alone. He is his own arbiter. He cannot rely on an acting teacher or a director to dictate or even guide him with his choices for building the character. While the instructor provides an environment where a myriad of choices can be made, it is the actor who must finally make these choices. He must create the mask character completely by himself. Taking this responsibility gives the actor the security that he has the ability and the technical means to do this again and again.

The job of the instructor is to create an environment in which actors can remove those blocks to their impulses and provide new routes to their sensory imaginations. The environment must excite and permit experience. It must be an environment which the actor completely trusts so that he will permit himself to take the necessary steps to open his instrument, his body, voice, and imagination. In his environment, the actor must be willing to let experiences occur without the full cognizance of where they are leading. If the actor is too self-critical before embarking, or if he needs complete justification and understanding of what the end results will be, the experience will be censored before it is absorbed. There must be respect for the fact that solutions will evolve from the doing: commitment is essential to the technique.

This book describes, defines, and discusses the mask characterization process, providing the theory behind the exercises and the step-by-step procedure in the organic development of the character from the mask. The manual is divided into two general parts: "The Instructor's Guide" and "The Actor's Guide." There is also an introductory chapter, "The Class Structure," which explains mask characterization procedures in the classroom. A sample class schedule may be found in the back of the manual.

In spite of the fact that this book is divided into separate parts for the instructor and the actors, I think it is important and highly beneficial for the actors to read the *entire* book before, during, and after the time of taking the class. The element of surprise in undergoing each step is less crucial than a total understanding of what will happen, what is happening, and what has happened to the actor as he experiences the characterization process. In my experience with the course, I have had several students take the class a second time. Their prior knowledge of the content in no way inhibited their learning. To the contrary, they were invariably more purposeful, focused, and thorough in their use of each exercise. They had a stronger sense of accomplishment and completion by the time the second character was formed.

One further note on the use of this book; I would suggest that the actor bring his copy of the book to every class session. Thus, he can use the questions in "The Actor's Guide," part 2, to stimulate his responses for the journal after each class working session.

I have employed the words actor, he, him, himself, in the interest of economy, as there is not yet a simple descriptive noun or pronoun in English to denote both genders. All quotations cited are taken from the journals of students who participated in the class.

This book is primarily a documentation of the class process Estelle Spector and I use in the course entitled Mask Characterization. However, the writing of the book has been largely assisted by several people who have given me numerous suggestions and editorial help. I would like to give special thanks to my friends Lenore Borzak, Laura Karp, and David Ravel for their excellent suggestions which I have incorporated into the text. I wish to also thank the students who generously loaned me their journals for the quotations cited.

Special acknowledgment must go to Christine Calomiris, my graduate assistant, who aided me on the preliminary drafts of the manuscript. Ms. Calomiris was a continual source of support, both with sentence construction and discussion of concepts involved in the characterization process.

I wish to express my gratitude to my husband, Paul Appel, the extraordinarily talented artist who created my masks.

A final massive amount of acknowledgment and gratitude must go to my friend Phylis Ward Fox. Her help in finding and defining the final form of this book is incalculable. I literally could not have completed this project without her.

Libby Appel
California Institute of the Arts
July 1981

Mask Characterization

Introduction:
The Class Structure

The Class Structure
"I have the luxury of time—time to work out my thinking—time to create my character."

If the only necessary step to this creative process was the initial burst of freedom experienced from covering the face, then the only mask necessary would be a paper bag or any simple cover. Further, if the only goal of the work was more extensive body and sensory involvement, then the same paper bag, or better yet, the neutral mask expressing the universal figure, would serve the purpose. However, this mask characterization process, akin to the role creation for a play, is a long journey in and out of the imagination to create a whole person, discovering and refining the behavior of that person in countless situations and periods of his life. This developmental process requires long work sessions, specific kinds of masks, a particular kind of space, and most of all, a disciplined commitment on the actor's part to fully respond to and explore creative impulses.

At first reading, the exercises described may simply seem to be basic, well-used improvisation techniques. They are that, of course, but coupled with the character masks and the order and speed with which they are administered, the exercises produce a much stronger effect on the actor's imagination and physical powers of endurance. They are designed to operate on two simultaneous levels: one, stripping away old personal limitations, and two, creating new layers of experience. The effects of the exercises are the compilation of deepening and developing concentration, sensory awareness, belief in imaginative circumstances, trust and relaxation so as to delve and explore immediate emotions, and the ability to build physical stamina and expand physical choices. This is a cumulative process, and it takes time, patience, and strength of will.

The Masks

Carefully designed character masks are required to achieve the best results from the process. The masks I use are full faces with features that are larger than life-size. They each have a mouth opening (covered with black gauze so that the actor's features cannot be seen behind it) large enough to permit sound and clear articulation. The fundamental characteristic of these masks is their contrary and ambivalent qualities. They do not express any one type of person or emotion. The features are purposely contradictory (one side of the mouth may droop, while the other moves upward, the brow is worried and the chin is defiant, etc.). This allows great width in interpretation for the actor and prevents the development of character "types" or stereotypes. The masks provide maximum inspiration while imposing few limitations.

While there are other kinds of material suitable to make masks, the artist used Celastic strips to make the masks and took them from a clay-form positive mold. They are painted to give a highly textured effect which combines with a subtle and rich mixture of colors. Although the masks are sophisticated in texture and color, they are primitive in style and expression. They are slightly grotesque and large, thus, there is an immediate need for the actor to *meet the size and depth of the mask, and decipher the ambiguity of personality*. Like any well-designed mask, they come alive only when filled with the actor's spirit and the actor's gesture.

Although the size of a group is optimally set at sixteen, I have twenty-five masks in order to provide each actor with greater range for selecting his own mask. Each mask is unique, but all twenty-five express a unity of style so that the characters belong in a similar world. The masks are all suitable for either males or females.

In some ways, the mask may be likened to a script. It is designed by an artist (as a script is created by a playwright) who developed the faces out of his personal imagination. Like a script, the mask provides some boundaries and definitions, although it is a great deal more flexible. It is a reference point for the actor. It is far more comprehensive than a neutral mask and yet far less rigid than a preconceived character mask such as those used for commedia dell'arte.

The Physical Space and Equipment

A permanent work area is needed. There must be adequate space for each individual to move freely. The average dance-studio classroom would be an excellent area in which to work. Mirrors on the wall (preferably with curtains so that at times the mirrors could be closed off from view) are an absolute necessity. The mirrors will be used daily whether the actor is working alone or is involved in group exercises. Hard sprung wood floors are preferable for extensive movement. Durable, lightweight chairs that can be stood upon, turned over, jumped on, run with, and sat on in every conceivable way must be in the room. Step units, small platforms or levels, and ladders are optional. Any objects that give the actor the opportunity to move in a different rhythm and position (up, down, across, under) are helpful. All equipment must be stored in a corner of the work area to permit a clear, open space for most of the session.

A stock of old clothing and costume pieces for men and women must be accumulated and stored for later use. This clothing should include items such as dresses, pants, shirts, nightclothes, capes, hats, belts, feathers, scarves, underwear, shawls, and any other exotic or ordinary item that is available. It should be from many possible eras and styles, fantastical and realistic. Costume departments and thrift shops are valuable sources for collecting these items. Keep them closed up in a container so that the actors do not see them until the appropriate time.

The work area should be kept absolutely clean. Actors must feel free to crawl and sprawl all over the floor and walls. Debris and dirt are not only dangerous to move around in but are also psychologically restricting. Every day a different actor in the group could be assigned to sweep the floor. This could be part of the physical warm-up.

The Psychological Space

"Work for yourself." "Stay in your own private space." "Use the space." These are admonitions that are continually a part of the side coaching of any exercise throughout the first half of the work process. They will not always be repeated with the directions for all the exercises described in this book, however, the actor needs to be reminded of these instructions during every exercise.

Since silence is required in the class, each actor, though working simultaneously with the rest of the group, is "alone" in his space, working for himself. There is almost a feeling that each individual exists in a vacuum. The character development process is a personal one, and one's concept of private, psychological space grows proportionately to the freedom one feels in the work. Students are encouraged not to talk about the class or their personal discoveries among themselves or with others outside the class. From this "isolation" comes a tremendous sense of relaxation; from this relaxation, the creative impulse is released and can then be expressed. The environment, therefore, must be clean, spacious, silent, isolated, and protective.

The Role of the Teacher

The role of the teacher in this process is, in a sense, nondirective. It is imperative that the instructor make no decisions for the actor and give as few opinions as possible about choices. There are *no right or wrong choices* for the development of the character. The only wrong choice is not to fill the choice or commit it completely to action. The teacher can remind the actor that his center has collapsed, that the actor is not making his idea clear or complete, or that the actor is staying too comfortable and not probing levels of character far enough or deep enough. It is the actor's responsibility to reach into his imagination to rid himself of trite behavioral patterns, to stretch deeper and further. The teacher must exhort the actor to FIND ANOTHER WAY, but it is best not to suggest that other way. Thus, a major function of the teacher is to provide an atmosphere physically safe but basically objective in which the actor can work without requiring immediate approval from any authority figure. The actor's discoveries are made through trial and error. If the actor is concerned about the instructor's opinion or evaluation, that dependency might prevent the actor from taking the risk to experiment. Responsibility to make clear, organic, meaningful choices is left in the hands of the actor. This leads to the development of the actor's confidence in trusting personal experience and resources to make decisions. The responsibility of the instructor, then, is to provide an atmosphere in which creation can take place. The instructor, although mostly noncommittal, is always there to protect the actors' physical space and guide them, when leading the exercises, to find their own discoveries.

Rules for the Students

The following is a list of requirements that must be made clear to the student before the masks are introduced:

1. *Silence.* There is absolute silence upon entering the classroom. All socializing occurs outside of the work area. You are alone once you have entered the room. If a question or comment is necessary, lift the mask off the face to speak. No one talks behind the mask until the character is developed and can speak for himself.

2. *Attire.* Leotards and tights (preferably black), bare feet, something to tie back long hair, and a sweater or wrap for quiet moments after the exercises are the required attire. Remove all personally identifying accouterments; jewelry, hair adornments, and bright, colorful clothing are not permitted. By stripping bare the actors' own personal decorations, the actor can develop new images of himself. The actor begins from a neutral state and wears no identifying clothing until the character emerges and begins to choose his own.

3. *Attendance and promptness.* Attendance at every session is re-

quired. Lateness is not tolerated. Students must work every session, even if they feel a little out of sorts. The mask can become a magic "cure," and further, the student can profit by bringing those depressed or queasy feelings of the moment to the day's session. Often, missing one session can feel like a strong rupture. The student has to then work hard at getting back into the rhythm of the next day's work. In addition, the exercises are cumulative and progressive. Missing out on a day's work is missing part of the layering process. When class is canceled because of school holidays or other occasions, the actors return to the mask with an extraordinary need to "get back." They grab their masks and rush to the mirror as if returning after a long, unwanted hiatus. It is, therefore, more advisable to keep on a steady, uninterrupted schedule right from the beginning.

The Journal

Each student is required to keep a journal charting the daily activities, discoveries, and feelings that occur in the class. This book must be a separate one from other notebooks or journals. It must be kept for the mask class alone and brought to every session. There is time allotted at the beginning and end of each session for the writing in the journal.

Since there is very little class discussion or explanation during the course of any day, the student is encouraged to write about any of his emotions and experiences as they happen. Because the actor cannot discuss or intellectualize the process with the group, he will enjoy delving into personal reactions alone with the journal. Once the character has evolved, the actor may find it useful to write in the journal occasionally with the mask on—to discuss his feelings as the character. Most of the time, however, the masks will be lifted when the actor writes in the journal so that he may clearly separate himself from his character.

The journal eventually becomes a record of the whole creative process of developing the character. It will always be a reference for the actor, an aid in comprehending his own experiential development. It is a record of the choices as they occurred and were later discarded or refined. These journals are never evaluated by the teacher. Therefore, the student is encouraged to be completely candid in expressing his own thoughts.

Warm-Ups

Upon entering the classroom, each actor does a physical warm-up. This is done silently and individually. It is the actor's responsibility to determine what exercises he needs to relax tension areas in order to focus concentration on his work. The warm-up is short, about five to seven minutes, because of the need to structure carefully class time and profitably utilize every minute. When the instructor is aware that the day's activities will be particularly strenuous, it is advisable to urge the students to stretch and shake out more vigorously than usual. The warm-ups continue to the end of the course.

Free Time

Immediately following the warm-up, actors pick up their own masks. It becomes a source of pride when an actor instantly picks out his "face" from the crowd of masks. They work alone with the masks, keeping their journals close by. They have free access to the mirrors in order to examine their physical changes. There is no structure. It is truly free time. The instructor is only an observer and a "security officer" if the occasion demands. At first, free time is very quiet. Actors choose small spaces near the mirror and look at themselves and the masks. Sometimes they never put the mask on at all. Some prefer to sit and think or to write in their journals. When the exercises begin to make demands, their bodies and imaginations loosen up considerably; this can easily be seen in their own free time activities. Since relationships are strongly discouraged in the structured exercises for a long time, the early interaction in free time is tentative as well. As the safety and trust behind the mask increases, the capacity to *play* comes forward. Before the characters evolve, there is a definite stage in which free time seems like a children's playground. This is a *necessary* development because it always leads to giving oneself greater permission to turn true feelings of the moment into motivations and actions.

As the class proceeds, free time seems to become more purposeful and productive, particularly as the actors make progress in the work process. However, it is imperative that the instructor always remain patient and removed, even in the earliest sessions. Feelings about the mask, the self, and other people are continually germinating and developing. Because there is no structure, interference, "suggestion," or approval/disapproval from the instructor, the actor can be free to behave at will.

Class Hours

One and a half to two hours are required for each work session. The class, as has been taught, meets three days a week for sixteen weeks. The plan of exercises as outlined in this book is based on that time framework. Variations, of course, are possible. However, personal discipline is necessary. In planning a class schedule, thought must be given to the fact that this process takes a great deal of time and total commitment. Every stage of development is a new discovery, and each new discovery needs time to be absorbed in order to be utilized later.

Thus, the creative atmosphere is constructed, and the "rules of the game" are set up. The atmosphere is one in which the actor can look at himself with great calm. It is one where he can operate with maximum freedom to rid himself of personality mannerisms and social images. It is a place where the actor is forced to take responsibility for his own actions, to make decisions, to explore and strengthen his reactions to stimuli, to get past overintellectualization which can inhibit the intuitive processes. With the framework of the class established, the actor can now risk his body and imagination more freely and fully in order to create a complete, totally realized character. He is now prepared to meet the mask.

Part 1:
The Instructor's Guide

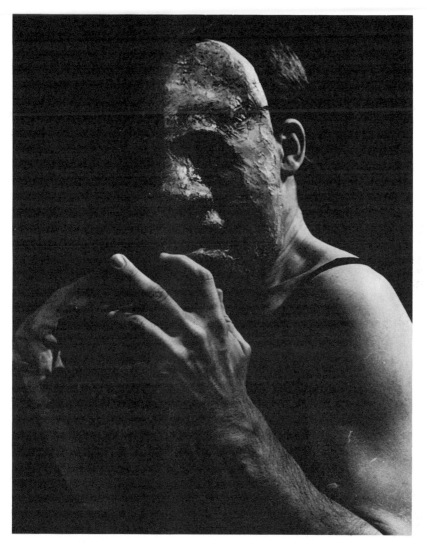

The Instructor's Guide
*"The mask lets so many of my normal defenses down that my
instincts just pour in."*

Encounter: Meeting the Mask

Encounter: Meeting the Mask
"Number 24 gives me a lot of energy. Very playful, sometimes manic, sometimes pathetic. Old, young—lots of range. Intelligent, dumb—I feel free working through it."

Step 1: First Encounter

On the first day of class, one mask is viewed. The mask is worn by someone who is not a member of the class, preferably a nonactor. I suggest
using a woman with fairly long hair. This allows for a distinct change in
the mask when the hair is rearranged around it. This person should not
attempt to "act" or demonstrate any attitude or emotion. She is simply a
model for the mask—a warm body to support the fixed face with reality
and substance.

TIME
Sixty to ninety minutes.

PURPOSE
To elicit from the group immediate impressions about the mask; to discuss the multidimensional possibilities found in the mask; to engage the
group in looking for and articulating specific feelings and impressions.

PROCESS
The model sits in a chair. Ask the class to observe the model and the mask
and—quickly without a great deal of thinking—volunteer comments. Encourage the students to look for particular features that elicit an impression. They must be specific. Have them look at the different angles of the
mask—walk around the figure, step back, step forward, step around. After
several minutes, instruct the model to walk around and make contact
with the actors. This exchange is done without verbal exchange between
actors and model. Now, instruct the model to change movement—to
walk faster, skip, run, jump, crawl, limp, hop, lie down, stand up. As the
model completes these instructions, encourage the actors to call out the
images and impressions that occur to them while watching the model.

OBSERVATION
During this first encounter, the group's initial comments will be general
(e.g., "grotesque," "strange," "primitive"). Then comments will become
more emotional (e.g., "*it's* so sad," "is *it* in pain?"). No sex is ascribed even
though the mask is on a female. Once the students have finished comment-
ing, several major principles will have come from this encounter:
    1. The mask is a mass of contradictions. The jaw could be determined,
the left brow forlorn, the nose delicate, the right brow cruel, one cheek
defiant, the other collapsed. The possibilities of personality are manifold.

No one attitude or emotion is communicated by the mask, no singular conception of the character is expressed, no stereotypes are possible.

2. Each individual in the group sees the face and its assemblage of contradictory parts differently. Yet, each individual is seeing a true picture of the mask according to his own understanding of people. Thus, there are *no right or wrong choices*. The mask is open to individual exploration.

3. The larger-than-life size of the mask forces the body to extend the physical action to meet that size. Small, subtle gestures must be very clearly and economically executed in order to be meaningfully communicated.

4. The personality traits of the character are prismatic. Since no one idea is communicated, the mask embodies numerous facets of a person. The goal, then, is to create a multifaceted, thickly layered character.

5. The immediate impressions of grotesqueness change to "exotic," "interesting," "different." The actors become intrigued by the challenge of stretching their ideas to meet the demands of this face.

6. Since the face is fixed, every change they see in it is communicated by the movement of the model. Thus, the necessity to settle the ideas, needs, and thoughts, and to make them strongly rooted in the body, becomes apparent.

With these principles articulated, ask the students to record their impressions in their journals. The questions in the student's section will refresh their memory of the actual event. Since this is the first day of class, it will be the only encounter when the journal is not in hand. However, the journal is to be readily available for all succeeding meetings.

Steps 2–3: Choosing the Mask

The selection of a mask with which the actor will work for sixteen weeks takes at least two sessions, four hours in total, with all the masks. If more than sixteen weeks are available for this process, it might be advisable to extend this to one more session. Whatever is decided, there should be a minimum of twenty-four hours between sessions to give the actors a chance to absorb and relax with their initial impressions.

PROCESS

1. The work space should be swept clean. There should be an ample number of full-length mirrors, small benches, chairs, or stools so the actors can sit, lean against, or stand on them.

2. Put the masks, individually identified by a number, on chairs placed against the wall.
3. Before the students enter the work area, the following instructions should be made clear to them:

Work alone. Do not talk to anyone.

Make a notation about every mask in your journal so that you may review these notes before making a choice.

Try to experience as many masks as you can, but be aware that you have another two hours in the next session to work with them. Be sure to work with all of the masks in these two days.

At the end of day two, you will be asked to put all masks back on the chairs, line up, and inform the instructor of your choice. Since your first choice may be taken by someone else, be prepared with at least five or six other possibilities.

Choosing the Mask
"Funny—It looks so different on her than on me. A lot of the masks do—in fact, all of them look different on each person."

Do not discuss your possible choices with anyone else in the class when you leave here today.

Put each mask on the chair you took it from when you are finished with it.

Work for yourself. Explore each mask to your own satisfaction. Take risks with the exploration so that your final choices will not come from your comfort zones. Try to keep your mind open to the mask. Let each one "talk" to you and challenge your imagination.

4. Before the actors leave that day, they should be reminded to review their notes, to prepare themselves to explore the remaining masks the second day, and to try to understand objectively how each mask already explored has affected them.

OBSERVATION

When the student enters the room, one sees why the length of time taken to choose the mask is absolutely mandatory. Soon after their entrance, the students' personal sense of time becomes disoriented. At the beginning of the session, they rush for the masks and work through three or four very quickly. After about thirty or forty minutes, they begin to realize that they have a great deal more time. They can permit themselves to slow down the exploration and spend more time with each mask. The atmosphere becomes less frantic and hurried; however, it is more intense. In addition, during the first session the sense of "play" is still quite tentative and inhibited. The student is not yet convinced that he is alone and that no one is watching. Sometimes movements are "performed," just in case someone might be looking. Students are still self-conscious about their bodies when they move at their own direction. Half the body is left out of an action. Journals are clutched close to the breast. The first attempts at physical statements are usually general attitudes, poses, and extended clichés. The working space each student takes is limited; a portion of the mirror and a small, personal territory is staked out. Before the session is over, not only are most actors engaged in choosing the face for which they will build a body and a personality, but they are also opening and rediscovering that victim of their adolescent cover-up—the imagination. Usually, it is difficult to give *of* yourself *to* yourself without a structure imposed by a teacher or a script. However, before long they begin to permit themselves to say "what if" and play in their own space. Toward the end of the first session, personal and meaningful explorations are just beginning. Actors start to imagine situations and play within the imagined circumstances. The actor's own face is examined next to a mask, and sometimes actors attempt to shape their own faces into the mask features. Masks are placed on other parts of the body, making the stomach or the rear end the face. When the masks are returned to the chair after these sessions, the faces of the actors will appear exhausted, as if they have been through a whole day of hard physical labor. This is the result of the intense concentration of private uncovering and discovering.

Final Choosing of the Mask

PROCESS
1. Actors repeat the explorations of step one.
2. At the end of the exploration, actors return the masks, assemble their notes and line up for the selection.
3. The masks are chosen in silence.
4. Each actor takes the mask he has chosen and sits alone with it. The remaining masks are taken away.
5. The remainder of the class is spent in private work. The actor records his thought and impressions as he sits with his mask. Instruct him to answer the questions provided in the actor's guide and extend beyond those questions to his own additional observations.

OBSERVATION
This session is calmer, more purposeful, right from the beginning. There seems to be a greater willingness to accept the responsibility to use time profitably and individually. The responses to the masks are stronger, slightly more emotional. The territory opens up and people look at themselves from varying distances in the mirror. The looking is more penetrating, and one feels the added electricity in the room. There are demand and command in the self-examination because each actor is intent on finding his particular face. Without any self-consciousness, the actor's involvement is so vital that one is suddenly aware of the strength of each one's *presence*—the quality that is so rare and illusive on the stage. (The teacher becomes heartened and hopeful that this presence will be able to be captured again as the work continues.) The actors are given a few minutes to return the masks and assemble their notes before they line up for the selections. There is concern at this point that there will be great disappointment and anger if one's mask is chosen by another. However, in spite of the tension and excitement in each person, there is civility in the room. They are each prepared with several other choices in case they

lose their first, and the rule of silence in the room seems to keep disappointment in check. Once the masks are chosen, the remaining masks are taken away, and the students sit alone with their own masks. They record what they felt during the past session as well as what they anticipate will happen with their new faces. With the selection of the mask, the actors have begun the long process of taking responsibility for making their own decisions. Their imaginations are stimulated, and it feels good and exciting. Focused concentration and the concept of working for yourself have been implanted in the actor. The isolation is already becoming protective. Each actor now begins to experience the freedom behind the mask.

Discovery: Opening and Stretching the Actor

Discovery: Opening and Stretching the Actor
"Discovery happens within me. Objects stimulate it, but it happens inside me when I am aware and open. I can feel it."

The process involves breaking down the restrictive physical and psychological barriers that inhibit the actor's thinking. The exercises are designed to help the actor relax behind the mask, to feel safe and alone, and to allow the mask to become a natural part of the body. Concentration and trust in *doing, responding*—not thinking—are developed. Physical stamina increases as the exhaustion begins to ebb. The ability to respond to and sustain imagery and new realities is vitalized. The instructor's images are only a starting point for the actor, who then stretches his own imagination to find unused, carefully stowed away sensory stimuli.

From the physical laboring, the actor learns to listen to and respect his own body. He is doing things that were never before logical, "right," or permissible because of his own laziness or fear of looking foolish. Out of these primary, unguarded, emotional responses, the actor will become aware of the *constants* in his behavior behind the mask—those reactions that seem to keep happening in spite of the change of circumstances. Thus, Discovery is a stripping away process in order to find those truths upon which to build the character.

Breaking in the Mask/Seeking Fundamentals

Th purpose of the Discovery period is to open up and stretch the actor's instrument (particularly his body and his imagination) so that he may call upon it to respond more personally and truthfully to the promptings of the mask. The exercises will eventually require the actor to use sound, and the Mask, when it is fully developed, will speak, but voice production and speech techniques are not the primary concern of this work and are minimally explored.

Discovery is a period of approximately five weeks, or fifteen two-hour sessions. It entails a series of exercises which increase in complexity and force the actor to use his innermost resources in simple, economical, uninhibited, and deeply instinctive ways. There is no emphasis placed upon creating the character or mastering any of the tasks. No one is looking at the actor and expecting him to do something right.

Step 4: Exploring the Room

TIME
Forty-five to sixty minutes for the exercise. Ten minutes for journal entry.

Breaking in the Mask/Seeking Fundamentals
"It took me a while to get used to the masks's being on my face, but now I hardly even notice it when I work."
"Behind the mask, I'm free. I look at people. I do my thing. I can make any noise I please, and when I want to react, I react."

PURPOSE

To allow the actor to explore the room and objects in the room; to begin to observe and explore the space through the mask he has chosen; to discover unexplored sensory reactions to objects; to arouse the actor's curiosity.

PROCESS

Set up the exercise with the following instructions for the actors:
1. Devise no stories.
2. Do not pretend to be anywhere else.
3. Create no sensory illusions.
4. Do not touch anyone's personal belongings.
5. Inspect the room.
6. Stack the chairs.
7. Climb the ladders.
8. Go up and down the step units in every way possible.
9. Explore the four corners of the room.
10. Move objects to other places in the room.
11. Use other parts of your body to move objects.
12. Go in and out the door.

SIDE COACHING

Explore objects with other parts of your bodies besides your hands. Use your feet, head, back, stomach, etc.

Change personal tempo in approaching objects; move more quickly or slowly.

Hop, roll, jump, to get there.

Change directions of approach; come at things sideways, backward.

Keep exploring. Really look and feel things.

Work for yourself.

Stay with anything as long as it interests you. When you are bored, move on to the next object at your own pace.

Look at color and texture.

Listen to the object.

Find out what interests you in the object.

Do not rest!

Keep your mind on your action!

NOTE

Repeat this exercise for fifteen minutes in the next class session before going on to Step 5.

Step 5: Looking at Yourself and Others

TIME
Forty-five minutes.

PURPOSE
To allow the actor to observe himself; to allow the actor to observe others.

PROCESS
Once free time has ended, the actor begins to inspect himself from all angles and positions. At the instructor's direction, he begins to inspect the other actors.

SIDE COACHING
Inspect yourself completely, from all angles and positions.
Inspect other people at will.
Listen to what you are looking at.
Take what you want. Stay with your object of exploration only as long as it interests you.
Use other parts of your body to explore.
Do not do anything to be social.
Work for yourself. Do not rest!
Challenge your sense to find more stimulation.

OBSERVATIONS
The explorations in Step 4, "Exploring the Room," have aroused the curiosity of the actor and permitted him to enjoy his own reactions to many objects. The actor will take this sense of freedom and the desire to explore into Step 5, "Looking at Himself and Others." He will feel fewer social compunctions about using the space, the objects, and the people around him. After these exercises the actor will be aware of what restrictions there are in breathing or seeing with the mask on. If there are problems, the mask should be adjusted using foam rubber on the inside between the actor's face and the mask.

Risking Balance/Flexing the Imagination

These exercises are designed to open the actor's body to other means of operation and to trigger sensory images that motivate his behavior. The involvement in the activities is a physical and sensory one; it is not an intellectual process. It requires increased stamina, stronger control of the body, and more concentrated belief in what you are doing. Once free time is over and the exercises begin, *there should be no stopping or resting during or in between exercises*. When the actor keeps moving, regardless of sore muscles or perspiration, there is no time or inclination to keep up or manipulate physical defenses. He truly gets past thinking. His body will submit to the image and take the risk with the movement, and he will suddenly find himself believing and doing things he has never considered before. The strenuous physical exertion will sometimes cause the actors to make accompanying vocal sounds to alleviate the tasks; they want to voice their sighs, grunts, and groans. For the time being, they should be cautioned to put the sound back into their bodies and to express their feelings through physical maneuvers and adaptations.

Upon completion of these specific exercises, the actor will begin to use his imagination constructively and specifically. The circumstances in the exercises are not strictly logical; however, they stem from a realistic, logical premise. The body must extend itself to meet the challenge of the circumstances. The actor will become aware of how to use his body more effectively and what blocks are in his way. Within the structure of each exercise set up by the instructor, the actor is free to fill in and respond to his own imagery.

Step 6: Picking Apples

TIME
Forty-five minutes or longer.

PURPOSE
To stretch and loosen the body; to awaken sensory images; to trigger physical impulses when sitmulated by images.

PROCESS
Instruct the masked actors to take a chair and bring it to a space on the floor. Once they are in their own space, instruct them to imagine a huge

Risking Balance/Flexing the Imagination
*"I'm beginning to understand the importance of movement for me.
I'm freeing my body, getting in touch with it. I sense a new
awakening in my work."*

apple tree in front of them and a basket next to the tree. Instruct them to pick the apples off the tree and place them in the basket.

SIDE COACHING
Use the chair to reach difficult places on the tree.
Risk your balance on the chair and reach for extremely remote spots.
There are thousands of apples on this tree, and you must pick so many of them. Get to the apples below and around the side.
Keep stretching.
Use different tempo rhythms. Move quickly. Slow it down.
Move the apples to another part of the room. Let the weight of the basket make you drop it. Pick it up again with another part of your body bearing the weight.

AFTER THE EXERCISE
Instruct the actors to move their chairs to another space on the floor with a part of the body other than the hands. They must find another way to get there without walking. They must do it quickly—without resting—without taking time to think. THIS INSTRUCTION IS GIVEN AFTER EACH EXERCISE. The actors must be constantly seeking new physical rhythms and different ways to propel their chairs and their bodies.

Step 7: Sitting on a Chair

TIME
Forty-five minutes.

PURPOSE
To explore an object with such intensity that the intellectual process stops and pure impulse takes over; to risk balance and discover new positions for the body to find comfort.

PROCESS
Instruct the actors to sit on their chairs in their space. When the instructor calls, "Change," they are to change position on the chair. They must find new ways to make themselves comfortable. They may change the position of the chair. They must work for themselves in their own space.

SIDE COACHING
(The changes begin slowly, but accelerate after about ten minutes.)
There are infinite ways to sit in the chair and make yourself comfortable. Find them.
Don't look around at others. Stay with your own imagination.
Don't go back to positions you have been in before.
Approach the chair from different angles.
Use different rhythms.
Use other parts of your body to "sit."
Allow yourself to find yourself in different situations.
Trust the fact that as soon as you get up and approach the chair again, you will know where you are and what you are doing. There is no need to think about it first. *Find it* once you are there. Don't anticipate where you are going.
The instant you are "comfortable," get up and start a new approach.

Step 8: Jumping on a Trampoline

TIME
Fifteen minutes.

PURPOSE
To strengthen imagery and feed it into a physical activity.

PROCESS
Instruct the actors to imagine a trampoline in front of them in their separate work spaces. Instruct them to feel it with their hands. Let the hands gently bounce. Then instruct them to place other parts of the body on the trampoline and have them bounce each part separately (feet, head, elbow, etc.). Next, have them climb on it and bounce with their whole body. Vary the height and rhythm of their bouncing. Lead with different parts of the body.

SIDE COACHING
Let the trampoline buoy you up. I know you are tired. Let it work for you. Let it relax those poor, exhausted parts of you.
Feel the vibration through your whole body, even though you are bouncing only one part of you.
Let the trampoline do the work. You don't have to make it bounce. Let it push you.

NOTE
Repeat this exercise in the next session when the actors feel fresh and energetic. Then continue to Step 9.

Step 9: Pulling a Rope

TIME
Thirty minutes.

PURPOSE
To strengthen imagery and feed it into a physical activity while isolating and stretching specific parts of the body; to suspend logical behavior and believe absurd circumstances.

PROCESS
Instruct the actors to do the following:
1. Stand on your chair in your space.
2. Start to pull in a heavy rope in front of you.
3. Feel the texture of the rope in your hands.
4. The rope is infinitely long and you will not come to the end of it no matter how much you pull.
5. Be aware of how your whole body operates to pull that rope. Understand and make a catalog of all your parts as you pull with your legs, back, neck, pelvis, etc. Put more of the effort into the body and take it out of the arms as you pull.
6. Pare the action down to the least necessary movement in order to get the job done.

SIDE COACHING
Pull the rope from the right side.
Pull the rope from the left side.
Pull from behind you.
Pull from below you.
Find other parts of your body to lead the pulling. Once you have pulled with one part; explore another possibility.
Risk your balance on the chair in order to pull.
Minimize the effort, maximize the pulling.

Step 10: Digging Stones and Feathers with a Shovel

TIME
Thirty to forty-five minutes.

PURPOSE
To strengthen imagery that is constantly changing and have specific parts of the body respond to the changing image; to increase concentration by having several sensory conditions to bombard the body's labor.

PROCESS
Instruct the actors to do the following:
1. In your work space, imagine you are standing on a mound of earth. In front of you is a shovel.
2. Pick the shovel up and begin to dig in the ground.
3. Adjust your body to the weight of the earth.
4. Use different parts of your body to exert pressure on your arms.
5. Push with your shoulders, your back, your stomach, etc.

SIDE COACHING
The earth is getting heavier. It feels like stones that you are removing from the ground. Adjust to the added weight.
Use another part of your body to dig because your arms must be very tired. Use your back to push the shovel, your legs, your neck.
The stones are getting lighter. They are like feathers now. Feel the change of weight and what adjustments your body makes to the change.
Notice how the feathers will fly away if you don't protect them with your body as you dig. Don't lose the feathers.
Protect them with another part of your body as you dig with still another part of your body.

Strengthening Concentration/Deepening Imagery

The next series of exercises present circumstances that will force a stronger focus of attention on solving the problems presented by the tasks. The sensory images are compounded and the conditions, always starting from a basic reality, are extended to a greater extreme than in previous exercises. They are experienced immediately following the last

Strengthening Concentration/Deepening Imagery
"I give in to (the instructor). I let her control the conditions for me, and then I can stretch myself farther than I thought."

group, and it is advisable not to stop for discussion or questions. All of the work in the Discovery period is cumulative. When each experience follows upon the other, the total effect is physical and emotional expansion. After these exercises, the actors will have a stronger realization that they must take the responsibility for increasing their concentration and intensifying their responses to imagery. They will know how far they have gone and how much further they can stretch themselves. They will be able to recognize for themselves how much more they must relax to get beyond physical limitations and censorial thinking.

Step 11: Pumping Water from a Well

TIME
Thirty to forty-five minutes.

PURPOSE
To intensify the image that feeds the physical activity; to strengthen the response to several images at one time; to get past logical circumstances.

PROCESS
Instruct the actors to do the following:
1. Imagine a bright sunny day—a perfect day for doing chores.
2. Imagine a pump with a well directly in front of you.
3. Start pumping for water.

SIDE COACHING
(In this exercise, the environmental conditions change radically. The student must adjust to each change while continuing the task of pumping.)
The sun feels delightfully warm on your body. Find the specific spot where the sun is warming you. Bask in it as you work.
Feel how the rest of your body is affected by the nice breeze.
The sun is getting hotter. Feel it beat down on specific parts of you.
The heat is very oppressive now. Feel how differently it makes you pump.
Don't stop the task, simply adjust to the heat.
The sun is taking away all of your energy, but you must keep pumping.
Use your back, your legs, underneath your arms, etc.
There is a breeze relieving the heat now. Feel it specifically touch parts of your body. It makes the task easier.
The sun seems to be going behind the clouds. Do not indicate your relief.

Take your feelings and put them into the work.
It is getting cooler now. Where is the breeze touching you?
It is sharp and cold. How is it affecting your work?
Do not rest. Keep pumping, but try and protect your body against the frigid wind.

Step 12: Sitting and Reading in a Chair

TIME
Thirty to forty-five minutes.

PURPOSE
To concentrate on two tasks without programming the next move; to take risks with the body without preconceived limitations.

PROCESS
Distribute a paperback book to each actor. Have each actor sit in a chair in his work space and begin to read the book. Instruct the actors in the following:
1. Get comfortable in the chair.
2. Begin to read the book. Really read; do not pretend to read.
3. Try to absorb what your are reading.
4. Do not skip around in the book. Take in every word.
After two to five minutes of reading quietly, the instructor will call, "Change." At that time the actor must change his position in the chair without taking his eyes off the book. He must keep reading and absorbing what he is reading. He must always keep in physical contact with the chair, even when he is changing his position.

SIDE COACHING
Don't take your eyes off your book.
Don't rest.
Don't anticipate your next move.
Keep your mind on your action, your reading.
Come at the chair without losing contact with it. Come at it from different angles, with different tempo rhythms.
Sit in every conceivable position.
Stretch yourself to sit and read in new ways.

Step 13: Hanging Pictures on a Wall

TIME
Thirty minutes.

PURPOSE
To place the student within a physical activity that forces him to extend his body beyond his programmed responses; to explore personal imagery (the images on the pictures); to experience absurd, yet believable, behavior.

PROCESS
Instruct the student in the following:
1. Imagine a wall in front of you.
2. On the floor of your work space are an infinite number of pictures of every conceivable size, weight, and shape. There are nails, tacks, a hammer, tape, all the tools you need to hang the pictures.
3. Start hanging them.
4. Use your chair to get to high places.
5. Try to find a specific image for each picture.

SIDE COACHING
Find a spot on the wall for every picture. It is a perfect day to get it all done. Find the imagery that excites you.
Reach all those out-of-the-way spots.
You might try the ceiling.
Balance yourself on the chair so as to get to those difficult places.
Put some on the bottom, next to the floor.
Leave no place unfilled.
Enjoy your task. This is fun.
Do not rest.
Oops, the picture up left is falling. Catch it, readjust it.
Oops, there goes the up center one. The one down right is falling at the same time. Get both of them quickly before they fall and bring down all the other pictures. Use parts of your body to hold them while you replace the tacks.
Oops, three are going down now—on the far right, below on the left, and right in the middle. Catch them.

OBSERVATION

The actors will note that in attempting to hold up two or three pictures at the same time, they had to hold themselves in awkward and absurd positions. These positions, though necessary for the task at hand, were probably humorous to watch. Thus, a sense of comedy is introduced without the actors feeling the need to "act funny."

Step 14: Setting the Table with Company Coming

TIME

Thirty minutes.

PURPOSE

To create and perform a task while allowing an outside environmental circumstance to affect the activity; to personalize the imagery (choice of music, tableware and accessories); to control every movement of the body with the use of slow motion.

PROCESS

Instruct the actor in the following:

1. Imagine a table and four chairs in front of you.
2. Imagine table linen, silverware, dishes, and all other accessories nearby. Be specific about what each piece looks like.
3. Collect the linen, silverware, etc., and bring it to the table.
4. Imagine that this is a marvelous evening, and that you want the table to look perfect for your guests.
5. Imagine a radio on. You are listening to some music while you work.
6. Begin to set the table.

SIDE COACHING

Let the music affect the way you work, always keeping your concentration on accomplishing the task.

Don't dance, just let the music affect the rhythm of your movement.

Change the music: waltz, rock, jazz, romantic tunes, etc. Be specific with the music you hear.

When the table is set, finish the last-minute details of the dinner in this area, moving to the music but keeping each detail of your task specific.

BRING EXERCISE INTO SLOW MOTION!

Keep working, but slow down all of your action. Keep the music running through you. You are in a time warp. Everything is exactly the same only it is very slow.

Get control of every small part of you: fingers, head movements, knee bends, etc.

You are in another time. Nothing is rapid or staccato. Go slower.

Slow it down even more.

Change the music to a lively tune. Keep the music's rhythm and the task going, but always in the slow time warp.

Return to normal time.

Catalog your muscles. Know how every part of your body is moving to perform these actions. Take this awareness into slow motion again.

Be specific. Get control. Be true to the music, the task, and your imagery.

Exploring Emotions

"Today I concentrated. I didn't want to—I tried not to. In the tunnel I didn't want to get scared, and I didn't want to let myself go. I told myself I was in a classroom, not a tunnel, but my body was in that tunnel and so I got there too. I was frightened and I cried. I cried when I was out of the tunnel too. This was because I was so determined to use my energy to get out of that tunnel."

Exploring Emotions

These next three key exercises are known as The Big Three. All of the principles set in motion during the previous exercises are combined in them: strong concentration, fulfillment of personal and specific imagery, response to deeply enmeshing physical and environmental conditions, extension of body behavior beyond logical realities. They are devices with sets of circumstances that heighten and condense crises: terrifying crisis and pleasurable crisis. Because the conditions are extreme, they trigger strong emotional reactions. The involvement in each experience is, as always, personal for every student, but the total effect is one of unlocking and allowing the emotions of the moment to physically lead the body. Later, these same exercises will be utilized to find physical centers that will cue other emotions, motivations, and behavior. This will be the first set of exercises in which the actors are encouraged to bring forth sound stimulated by the activity. Up to this time, when heavy breathing, sighing, or straining sounds came out of the activities, the student was to put the breath and the sound back into their bodies to give them more fuel for the task. Now this sound is to be permitted.

The accumulation of the exercises through Step 17 will provide numerous benefits. From the duration of hard physical labor and the necessity to get past the feelings of exhaustion, comes a sense of stamina and renewed confidence in the body's power. The constant urgency to use the body fully and economically, in hitherto unimagined ways, triggers the sense of discovery of physical resources. The reliance upon and the specification of imagery enriches the sensory imagination. The actor no longer "indicates" inner and environmental sensory conditions. He has learned to allow the image to be set in motion and to simply respond to it. Rich sound is expressed from the center of the body in the midst of crisis. It is relaxed and true sound, not tightened and unfocused. Emotions are flowing as parts of one's self are being exposed and explored. From the emotional surges, whether painful, defiant, determined, pleasurable, or liberating, the actor learns to retain them in the body and use them as a source of energy to propel him forward. Thinking too much is minimized, and as a result, more experiences are personally realized. The inventory of muscles produces an intense ordering process in which the actor becomes increasingly aware of how to understand and control the operation of his body. The instructor will have tangible evidence of these benefits when observing the students in free time. Invariably, at this point, the actors are more open physically. They dare more by themselves and with others. They explore the mask more thoughtfully, looking for evidence in the mask of their newfound personal discoveries. There is total safety in isolation now.

Step 15: Crawling in a Tunnel

TIME
Forty-five minutes. The exercise is divided into three parts.

PURPOSE
To cause strong emotional response from the circumstances; to use the emotional response as an energy center to propel the body as it moves.

PROCESS
(Part 1)
Instruct the actors in the following:
1. Imagine a cave in your work space directly in front of you.
2. There is an opening in this cave.
3. Get into the cave and start to explore its texture as you move forward.
4. It is cool but not cold.
5. The texture of the surface is pleasant to touch.
6. Allow the images to take over your mind. This is an adventure. Crawl and explore.

SIDE COACHING
The tunnel is narrowing as you proceed forward. Your head and shoulders feel the narrowing before the rest of your body does. Adjust to the difference.
The air is getting colder and the surface of the tunnel is getting damp. Keep going forward.
There is a turn to the right. Negotiate your body around the turn.
It is narrower now. Keep minimally small as you move or you will be scratched by the walls all around you. Keep your head down. Make your shoulders small as you move, or you will be scratched by the walls all around you. Keep your head down. Make your shoulders smaller, tighten your buttocks to get through.
A left turn now.
It is dark and clammy, almost slimy. The situation is desperate, but there is no turning back. You must get to the end of the tunnel.

If sound is happening in your body, allow it. Let it help you move forward.

Use the sound.

Stop! You have come to a dead end. The tunnel stops here. Crawl backward to the fork in the road. You must go back. There is no other way out. At the fork in the road, readjust your body to make the turn into the other side of the fork.

It is terribly cold, disgustingly slimy, and very narrow, but you must get out. Keep going.

Use the sound.

There is a light. Do you see it? Way in the distance? Crawl to it. Hurry. Watch your head, your shoulders, your back. Don't lift your legs. You have got to get out.

Let the sound out.

Be aware of your body as you make this final burst of energy to freedom. You have reached the end. Pull yourself up.

PROCESS
(Part 2)
Continue to instruct the actors with side coaching.

SIDE COACHING
Allow the final spurt, when you were crawling to the light, to infuse your body when you are on your feet. Don't lose the sound.

Move forward. Feel which part of your body is pulling you forward. Is it your shoulders? your head? your chest? your pelvis? Where is the major thrust forward centered? *Let that center lead you around the room.* Walk.

Keep the sound.

Make an inventory of your muscles as you move.

Stop. Lift your mask. Shake out.

Put the mask back on. Now, go back again to that same movement. If you lose the center of the thrust or the feeling, go back on to the floor and re-create the last moments of the struggle.

PROCESS
(Part 3)
Continue to instruct the actors with side coaching.

SIDE COACHING
Keep walking with the same lead in your body, but change the rhythm. Move slowly. Quickly.

Look at yourself in the mirror as you move. Your emotions will change.
Let them change, but keep the same center from the tunnel.
Run to catch a bus. Run, run.
Oh, you missed it.
Lie down on the floor with what you feel.
Walk in and out of the doors.
Take a chair. Move it to a space in the room. Sit down with what you feel.
Look at other people.
Keep the sound running through you.
Go over and shake someone's hand.
Go back to your chair.
Now, go to your journals, keeping this energy center propelling you. Sit with it. Pick up your journal. Lift your mask and write down what you have just experienced.

AFTER THE EXERCISE
Have the actors repeat the walk discovered from the last burst out of the tunnel several times, carefully noting any changes of emotions, changes in breathing patterns, and how all the parts of their body are fitting into this central pattern of energy. Move in slow motion to maintain complete control.

Step 16: Flying a Kite

TIME
Forty-five minutes. The exercise is divided into three parts.

PURPOSE
To allow the images to move the actor instead of the actor controlling the images; to create a pleasurable response from a set of circumstances; to move with the emotional energy from that response.

PROCESS
(Part 1)
Instruct the actors in the following:
1. Imagine yourself outside on a lovely day. The air smells sweet. Gentle but firm breezes are blowing.
2. You are in an open field with no obstructions anywhere.

3. You have designed and constructed the kite in front of you. Be specific about its shape, colors and design.
4. Pick up the kite in front of you, and let it fly. Run with it.

SIDE COACHING
This is a perfect day for flying a kite.
Make the kite do wonderful tricks in the sky.
Move your body to manipulate the kite.
The air is so perfect that it is now moving your kite for you. You don't have to *do* anything.
Let the kite lead you. Let it pull you around. It is a pleasure. It is an easy pull and push.
It's so nice. In fact, *you are one with the kite*. Let go of the kite because you are now up in the sky being cushioned by the clouds, being tossed by the breeze.
Let the clouds hold you. Lean on them. Rest on them.
Risk your balance and trust that they will hold you.
LET THE IMAGE WORK FOR YOU. DON'T PUSH THE IMAGE.
Don't "dance."
Allow the sound to come from within you.
Trust the image to move you.
The clouds are caressing you, holding you, touching you behind your head, under your arms, between your legs, under your feet, etc.
Let yourself tumble down into the clouds on the floor. Control all your parts as you spiral down.
Allow the sound to come through your whole body.
Respond with your body to the clouds as they caress you.
Don't rest.
React with each separate part of you and the sound to the touches and soft caresses. Enjoy it. Give yourself to it.
Stand up in slow motion, in this time warp, and move forward, still being held and caressed by the clouds and the breezes.
Change to normal time and find the center from which the pleasurable energy is coming.
Use that part to pull you forward.
Catalogue the rest of your body as you walk.
Change your tempo rhythms.

PROCESS
(Part 2)
Continue to instruct the actors with side coaching.

SIDE COACHING
Allow the final spurt, when you were walking in slow motion, being held and caressed by the clouds and the breezes, to infuse your body as you move. Don't lose the sound.
Move forward. Feel which part of your body is pulling you forward. Is it your shoulders? your head? your chest? your pelvis? Where is the major thrust forward centered? *Let that center lead you around the room.* Walk.
Keep the sound.
Make an inventory of your muscles as you move.
Stop. Lift your mask. Shake out.
Put the mask back on. Now, go back again to that same movement. If you lose the center of the thrust or the feeling, go back onto the floor where you first tumbled into the clouds, feeling the reaction of the different parts of your body, allow yourself to be pulled up and sense where the center of your body is as you begin to walk around again.

PROCESS
(Part 3)
Continue to instruct the actors with side coaching.

SIDE COACHING
Keep walking with the same lead in your body but change the rhythm.
Move slowly. Quickly.
Look at yourself in the mirror as you move. Your emotions will change.
Let them change but keep the same center from tumbling in the clouds.
Run to catch a bus. Run, run.
Oh, you missed it.
Lie down on the floor with what you feel.
Walk in and out of the doors.
Take a chair. Move it to a space in the room. Sit down with what you feel.
Look at other people.
Keep the sound running through you.
Go over and shake someone's hand.
Go back to your chair.
Now, go to your journals, keeping this energy center propelling you. Sit with it. Pick up your journal. Lift your masks and write down what you have just experienced.

AFTER THE EXERCISE
Have the actors repeat the walk discovered from tumbling in the clouds several times, carefully noting any changes of emotions, changes in

breathing patterns, and how all the parts of their body are fitting into this central pattern of energy. Move in slow motion to maintain complete control.

Step 17: Rowing a Boat

TIME
Forty-five minutes. This exercise is divided into three parts.

PURPOSE
To deal with a life or death crisis; to move with the energy center of the emotional response to the crisis.

PROCESS
(Part 1)
Instruct the actors in the following:
1. Imagine yourself in a rowboat on a sunny day.
2. The rowboat is tied to the dock.
3. Feel the sun touch you on specific parts of your body.
4. Dangle your hands and feet in the water if you like.
5. It is so pleasant. A little breezy, but not uncomfortable.
6. Feel the gentle rock of the boat as the water moves it. Rest and enjoy the sensations.

SIDE COACHING
It's getting a little windy, but there's no danger because you are tied to the dock. Feel the boat rock more vigorously.
Sit up. You seem to have drifted way out to sea. The boat must not have been properly tied.
The wind is very strong now, and it is pulling you farther and farther from shore. In fact, you can barely see the shore. You had better engage the oars and row back to shore.
The water is very choppy and the boat is drifting rapidly out to sea. Row hard. Row against the wind and the churning sea.
Allow the sound to help you pull against the sea.
Use all your strength.
Use another part of your body to push the oars so that you can get more power.
Water is coming into the boat. Bail it out with one hand.

Oh, you lost an oar. Grab the oar that is left and push, pull against the storm.

You are now in the eye of a terrible storm.

Use another part of your body to row as you bail out the overflowing, dangerous water. Keep changing parts.

The other oar is loose. It is gone now. Use your arms. Get back to shore. Push against the water. Push.

Get to your feet and move forward with this surge against the sea in your body.

Keep your sound.

Inventory all parts of your body as you move forward.

PROCESS

(Part 2)

Continue to instruct the actors with side coaching.

SIDE COACHING

Allow the final surge against the sea in your body to infuse your body as you move. Don't lose the sound.

Move forward. Feel which part of your body is pulling you forward. Is it your shoulders? Your head? Your chest? Your pelvis? Where is the major thrust forward centered? *Let that center lead you around the room.* Walk.

Keep the sound.

Make an inventory of your muscles as you move.

Stop. Lift your mask. Shake out.

Put the mask back on. Now, go back again to that same movement. If you lose the center of the thrust or the feeling, go back onto the shore where you were struggling against the wind and water, feeling the reaction of the different parts of your body. Now, allow yourself to be pulled up and sense where the center of your body is and begin to walk around again.

PROCESS

(Part 3)

Continue to instruct the actors with side coaching.

SIDE COACHING

Keep walking with the same lead in your body but change the rhythm. Move slowly. Quickly.

Look at yourself in the mirror as you move. Your emotions will change. Let them change, but keep the same center from the final surge against the sea.

Run to catch a bus. Run, run.
Oh, you missed it.
Lie down on the floor with what you feel.
Walk in and out of the doors.
Take a chair. Move it to a space in the room. Sit down with what you feel.
Look at other people.
Keep the sound running through you.
Go over and shake someone's hand.
Go back to your chair.
Now, go to your journals, keeping this energy center propelling you. Sit with it. Pick up your journal. Lift your masks and write down what you have just experienced.

AFTER THE EXERCISE
Have the actors repeat the walk discovered from the pull to shore several times, carefully noting any changes of emotions, changes in breathing patterns, and how all the parts of their body are fitting into this central pattern of energy. Move in slow motion to maintain complete control.

Finding Centers
"At sixteen I wasn't nearly so afraid of death, and the struggle seemed energetic. At this age there really seemed to be springs under my feet. I know what it feels like to carry what I am feeling into my body."

Finding Centers

Every person operates from a center. It is the central point around which the carriage and alignment of the rest of the body is organized. Along with inherited physical characteristics, a person's individual psychological and environmental influences play a large part in how he moves and holds himself. If one is uptight and inhibited, the center might be in raised, tightened shoulders, with accompanying indrawn arms, rigid spine, and stiff legs. If one is sensually and sexually hungry, the center might be in the groin, with the rest of the body following behind the pelvic thrust that leads the forward motion.

The center often literally leads the body when the individual moves. Heads that are centers (perhaps because of unloved, unwanted bodies) push forward as the rest of the body is left drooping behind. Sometimes the center is "hidden," as with a tightened stomach (from "Hold your stomach in. Be a good girl."), causing the shoulders to slouch forward to lead the movement. Whether the center leads the body or not, the actor will find he will have a different sense of self with each new center. When one organizes one's body around a central point, there is a change of personal rhythm, a different style of movement, an altered breathing pattern, a different lead and manner of walking, reclining, and sitting. These *physical changes will affect the way an individual thinks*. Characters will begin to emerge from finding new centers and reordering the body alignment accordingly. These centers are *organic*; they come out of experiences in which the actor's emotional responses are conditioned by his body's actions. They are *behavioral*; they come out of the way he thinks and feels. It is not the same thing as putting on a funny walk or affecting a particular posture or pose. It is a complete ordering of the physical parts of the body to fit the emotional and psychological "middle" of the character's existence. Even though the actor's body is made up of the same "ingredients" as the character—the same height, weight, overall shape—the center will be different. Thus, the character will look, feel, think, and behave differently from the actor.

The following exercises are designed to aid the actor in locating numerous centers with their accompanying physical organizational patterns. Steps 18–20 aid in the foundation of these exercises by recalling the physical and emotional responses experienced when creating the tasks of crawling through a tunnel, flying a kite, and sitting in a rowboat. The actor will recall the specific burst of energy from the specific task, take inventory on where it centered in the body, and then begin to walk with that energy awareness placed in the specific part of the body affected. He will then be ready to increase his discovery with more complicated tasks allowing him to perfect that center he has organically created. Steps 21–29 will allow the actor to experience eight new centers. Steps 21–25 repeat the tunnel, kite, and rowboat exercises with additional sensory imagery, thereby changing the emotional conditions and creating a new center of energy for each exercise. Steps 25–29 will offer a different exercise to assist the actor in locating other centers in his body. It is important that each time a new center is discovered from experiencing these exercises that it be tested in routine behavior—sitting, walking, running, leaning, greeting other people (see parts 2 and 3 of Step 15— "Crawling in a Tunnel"). In this way the actor has the opportunity to experience the many new feelings and thoughts that spring out of each physical center.

Steps 18–20: Re-creating the Centers of Crawling in a Tunnel, Flying a Kite, and Rowing a Boat

TIME
Each exercise follows the same procedure and lasts fifteen minutes.

PURPOSE
To re-create centers previously discovered in past exercises; to strengthen the actor's recall ability.

PROCESS
These instructions are followed for creating each of the centers previously discovered.
1. Re-create in your mind the last burst of energy experienced in the exercise with (the tunnel, flying a kite, or rowing a boat).
2. Place that energy into your body and begin to walk recalling the center which developed from that experience.
3. Re-create the sound which developed from that experience.
4. Pass the mirror and check yourself as you move.
5. Take a chair, sit down. Then approach the chair from different angles to sit for different reasons.
6. Lift the mask. Shake out.

NOTE
After one center is re-created, have the students shake out and go on to the next center to be recalled. This will take thirty to forty-five minutes of one

session. Then the students are ready to use the three exercises (tunnel, kite, boat) to discover other centers from added conditions to the given circumstances.

Step 21: Using a Score

TIME
Twenty to thirty minutes.

PURPOSE
To experience a new center; to permit an age to alter the behavior when the center is located; to take responsibility for choosing an exercise and work at the actor's own pace and direction.

PROCESS
The instructor reviews with the actors the given circumstances and movement directions (physical actions) of the tasks of crawling through a tunnel, flying a kite, and rowing a boat. These directions are called the *score of actions*. Each actor is instructed to choose and work on one of these scores at his own pace and direction. When the group reaches the climax of their *separate* scores, they must get to their feet and move. If there are a few actors ready earlier, they should keep walking with their last burst of energy centered in the body until the rest of the group is on its feet. The instructor gives the following directions to the actors:

1. Choose one exercise from crawling in a tunnel, flying a kite, or rowing a boat.
2. Review the physical score of the circumstances for the one you select.
3. Lie down on the floor.
4. Release all your tension from specific areas of your body until you feel completely relaxed.
5. Pick a number from fifteen to seventy-five.
6. Breathe in that number with every inhalation and feel it go out with every exhalation.
7. Take the number all the way through your body as you feel your breath travel to every location inside your body.
8. Feel it in your toes, your finger tips, your ears, the small of your back, etc.
9. Concentrate on no other thought but the inhalation and exhalation of the number.
10. When you are ready, bring yourself to a position to begin your selected score.

11. *The number is now your age.* Do not "play" the age.
12. Trust the fact that the age has been breathed into every part of your body.
13. Begin your score. Do not generalize the struggle or the imagery. Keep the circumstances specific and real.
14. Do not anticipate where each step will take you.
15. Work at your own pace, thoroughly and specifically, experiencing each step of the score.
16. Allow the movement to bring a sound out of you.
17. When you are on your feet and walking, keep the sound and take a careful inventory of the center and the rest of your body.

After these instructions have been given, begin the side coaching of parts 2 and 3 of the tunnel exercise (see Step 15) with the following additions:

1. Have the actor pass the instructor and direct the sound to the instructor.
2. Have the actors go to their journals with what they have in their body. Lift the mask. When they are writing, they are to describe the physical center that propelled them and the accomanying organization of the body. Examine how they felt and thought about themselves operating from this center. Examine what the age did to the experience.

Step 22: Using a Score with Specific Inner-Sensory Condition and/or an Environmental Condition

TIME
Twenty minutes.

PURPOSE
To increase the sensory conditions and thus change the feelings that ensue from the crisis; to experience a new center; to take responsibility for one's choices; to increase concentration on several levels of imaginary input.

PROCESS
Repeat the same procedure as in Step 21, with the following additions:

1. The actors may stay with the same score—either the tunnel, the kite, or the boat, or they may change. Encourage them to seek an experience that will continue to stretch their imagination and challenge their physical limitations.
2. Encourage the actors to make their choice more difficult—a new age, a more unknown environment, more contradictory conditions.

3. Instruct them to breathe in a different number between fifteen and seventy-five.
4. Instruct them to decide on an inner-sensory condition and/or an environmental condition. These conditions do not have to be appropriate to the task (e.g., flying the kite in a rainstorm with a rash on one's hands). The choices now become the actors. Encourage them to use every opportunity to stretch their imaginations to the fullest.
5. When the sound begins to develop, have the actor form it into a word and call it to the instructor as he passes by. The word may be a nonsensical one.
6. Have the actor take a chair and find a space for himself. When he is sitting, instruct him to look at other people.
7. Have the actor call out his word to other people and respond to others calling to him with their word.

Steps 23–25: Using a Score with a Specific Location

TIME
Each exercise takes twenty minutes.

PURPOSE
To increase the sensory conditions for finding a new center; to find oneself in imaginary locations and deal with the circumstances.

PROCESS
Repeat the same procedure as Steps 21 and 22 with the following additions:
1. Have the actors choose a specific location, a new sensory condition, a new number between fifteen and seventy-five.
2. The location selected should not be familiar to the actor.
3. Encourage the actor to use his imagination and select a location and time frame he might not know anything about (e.g., crawling in an Indian cave on a hot, muggy day in the West Virginia Hills at thirty-five years of age. Or, rowing a boat on the Black Sea in Russia with a hangover at sixty-five years of age).
4. When the sound becomes a word, have the actor commit to it not worrying about whether it sounds foreign or strange.
5. Have the actor make contact with another person. Have him shake hands, dance, hug that individual.

NOTE
Each time the exercise is repeated, instruct the actor to change his circumstances, location, and inner-sensory condition. Encourage him to be very specific, and go through the chosen score of actions thoroughly each time so that he will not anticipate the discovery of the energy center when the crisis is at its highest point.

OBSERVATION
The time to get through the given circumstances and scores of actions with each of the preceding exercises, Steps 21–25 will decrease. The actor makes this adjustment without the need for instruction. He simply moves to the climax or strongest crisis moment of the circumstances quite swiftly and takes the energy center to his feet and finds a normal routine of walking, running, leaning, sitting, climbing, etc. Continue to encourage the actor not to anticipate where he will center the energy in his body. The center must always organically come from the experience of the exercise.

Step 26: Doing a Private Task

TIME
Thirty to forty-five minutes.

PURPOSE
To locate and move with a new center; to change one's thinking and one's behavior while operating from this new center; to expand belief in absurd circumstances.

PROCESS
Instruct the actors in the following:
1. You are alone, with your chair, in your own place.
2. Choose an imaginary place.
3. You are doing a personal chore (e.g., painting your fingernails, washing your hair, shaving, clipping your toenails).
4. Use a tool for your chore (nail clippers, shampoo, bottle of polish, etc.).
5. This task will take a long time so do not expect to finish it before the exercise is over.
6. It is an excellent evening to get this job done, and you are completely alone, so you can relax and enjoy your task.

SIDE COACHING

As you work, make the tool grow a little larger and heavier. Adjust yourself to the size and weight.

It is even larger and heavier now.

Keep expanding the size and weight until you must completely realign your body to hold the object. Don't let that disconcert you. You can make the adjustment.

The object is now absolutely enormous, and you must continue to work with it.

Oh dear, someone is watching you. Feel the eyes on some specific part of you. Adjust your body to avert the eyes. Do you need to cover yourself? Do you want to flaunt your absurd, private behavior with the enormous object? Keep working, but adjust to the loss of privacy as you work.

That someone won't go away. Pick your object up and carry it to another place in the room. Try and hide it from that person's eyes as you move. I know it is huge and cumbersome, but you can find a place for it.

Shift it to another part of your body.

Try still another part as you attempt to hide it.

It is impossible to hide so put the object inside you. *Now assume the tool is in your body.* Readjust your body to the shape of the tool, and where you placed it is your center. If your center is wobbly and round like a cake of soap or long and pointy like scissors or a razor, what does it do to the rest of your body? Move with this center. Sit with it.

Change your tempo rhythm.

Catch the bus.

Lean.

Go in and out the door.

Go and sit on a chair and start to do your original task but keep your body adjusted to this center.

Now go to your journal and pick it up with what you have in you.

Steps 27–29: Doing a Private Task with Specific Circumstances

TIME

Twenty to thirty minutes for each exercise.

PURPOSE

To challenge oneself to find new centers not yet explored.

PROCESS
Repeat Step 26 with the following variations:
1. Change the task.
2. Change the placement of the body when the object is hidden.
3. Increase the weight and size of the object before moving it around the room.
4. Deal realistically with the growing absurdities of the situation and the task.
5. If you find your torso always becomes rigid when the tool is placed inside your body, choose an activity and tool which will probably change your rhythm and movement (e.g., shampoo or soap or a washcloth, which will be soft and mobile once placed inside your body).

NOTE
Once using a score and doing a private task have been completed, do two more rounds of these exercises. Have the actors choose whether they will do a score (tunnel, kite, or boat) or a private task. Encourage them to make decisions that will continue to challenge their body and imagination with unique and exciting choices. Challenge them to try to explore every possible body center and behavior from those decisions. The accumulation of these experiences with many different centers of energy will aid the actor in uncovering the character at a later point in the work process.

Finding Form and Economy

Now that the body is working more expressively, it is time to clarify these physical and emotional statements. The body must be trained to communicate the thoughts economically. There must be a beginning, middle, and end to each statement. In other words, the image and thought must be full on the inside, and the form in which they are communicated must be clear and controlled on the outside. The actor must begin to be aware that a raw primary impulse must be given form and shape. Every idea, even if it is abstract, must be contained within a communicative shape.

After these exercises have been completed, the Discovery period is "officially" at an end. However, the discovery of self and mask go on until the last day of the work. At this point in the process, each actor has truly discovered that he has an active imagination, and he can trust it to vitalize the body and use it constructively and specifically to communicate

Finding Form and Economy
"We all got into the game of it. The initial impulses can always be cleaned up to express the phrase. As we went further, the cleaning up got faster and faster for me. Each part of my body moved in a specific way till the end of the statement."

feelings and ideas. Each actor can now listen to his body and trust it to cue different emotions. Without forcing discoveries, he can locate centers. He has experienced the *doing* moment by moment, and can trust the creative impulse that inspired the action. The body will now meet the demands of the mask. The exercises have been long and laborious, but they have permitted relaxation and freedom to get to the actor's inner core. The instructor has manipulated some of the experiences, but this has not been inhibiting. It has given the actor the opportunity to be alone. The structure has been protective, to provide the freedom to explore the body and the imagination in the widest range possible. The actor is alert to his behavior, and he knows when it is organic—a truthful extension of what is happening inside. All of this work is the foundation for developing the character with the mask.

Step 30: Making Your Body Speak

TIME
One hour.

PURPOSE
To tap immediate impulsive associations between words and physical statements; to take the impulse through the entire body so that the whole actor is involved in the word; to make clear, economic, physical statements of words.

PROCESS
Instruct the actors in the following:
1. When I call out the following words or phrases, instinctively react to them.
2. Make a nonverbal, physical statement that is expressive of the word or phrase.
3. Do not try to "indicate" or "dance" the meaning.
4. The expression may be abstract, but it must fully go through the whole body.
5. Once you have found the statement, clarify it so that it is simple, with a beginning, middle, and end.
6. Do it for the whole group.
7. Act immediately, without thinking, and then refine the movement.

NOTE
When this exercise is done, feel free to add words and phrases as time permits. Redo each one until clarity and economy are reached. These are quick and fun to do. Coming after all the previous work, actors will be more daring and impulsive with their choices.

SIDE COACHING
(These are suggested words and phrases.)

Hello.	I like you.
Yes.	Good-bye.
No.	You are sexy.
Please.	Who are you?
Can I help it?	Don't touch me.
My foot itches.	Hold me.
I dare you.	I'm in pain.
God damn it.	Give me a hand.
Why are you crying?	I'm bored.

Step 31: Doing a Simple Action

TIME
Thirty minutes

PURPOSE
To clearly and economically express an objective (active verb) with the whole body.

PROCESS
Instruct the actors in the following:
1. From the first impulse choose a simple sentence with an action verb. (Example: I want to jump rope. I need to pee. I must shine my shoes.)
2. Make a nonverbal physical statement with this action.
3. Have a beginning, middle, and end.
4. Do it simply, economically, with total body commitment.
5. Hone away any actions that are unnecessary. When you are finished, the statement will be shown to the whole group.

Step 32: Doing a Simple Action with an Obstacle

TIME
Thirty minutes.

PURPOSE
To find a solution to an objective that is burdened with an obstacle in a simple, clear, economic series of movements.

PROCESS
Repeat the same procedure as Step 31 with the following addition: an obstacle. (Example: I want to jump rope, but the rope is too short.) Choose a new action verb.

Step 33: Doing a Simple Action with an Absurd Obstacle

TIME
Thirty minutes.

PURPOSE
To permit the suspension of logical circumstances in order to exercise imaginative choices to solve the problem.

PROCESS
Repeat the same procedure as for Step 32 with the following addition: an *absurd* obstacle. (Example: I want to jump rope, but the ground is made of gooey cream cheese.) Choose a new verb.

NOTE AND OBSERVATION
Steps 32 and 33 should be repeated if there is time in the schedule. The students enjoy working with these objectives, and the more they do them, the freer they will become to find imaginative solutions to the problems. These simple action exercises, along with Step 30, "Making Your Body Speak," can be graphic demonstrations to the students as to how far they have come in using parts of their bodies and imaginations to make physical statements that have hitherto been untapped. The students should be encouraged while watching others to react to each other's exercises with physical expressions that are full and energetic.

Development: Finding the Character

Development: Finding the Character
"How much is the mask affecting me, and how much am I affecting the mask? Who is this character anyway?"

The exercises for the next four weeks, ten to twelve sessions, are primarily focused on identifying and solidifying the character from the mask. Up to this time, there has been no emphasis placed on finding a specific character. To the contrary, actors have been urged to keep very open, to relate to every possible stimulus, and to give themselves every possible experience so that the development of a character will emerge from a rich range of emotions and behavior. The mask has almost seemed superfluous, simply the covering to aid and abet the uncovering. While most of the class time has been used for the discovery exercises, free time has been continuing and paralleling the work process each day. Individual, private discoveries with the mask have been encouraged. While the full meaning of the constant and continuing patterns is not always immediately accessible to the actor, the recurring feelings, thoughts, and physical actions have been noted in the journals.

Now it is time to analyze the discoveries already made and to test and search for new possibilities in order to solidify a foundation for the character. One of the best ways to know who you are is to see yourself reflected in someone else's eyes. It is time to explore relationships with people, objects, and places. The decisions for the character will subsequently emerge. When these decisions emerge, the character begins to take form. Initial decisions about the past and the present are firmed. Each character has a spine: a psychological and physical center. From this center, the character's true vocal tone and speech pattern are revealed. The actor will then be ready to commit to filling the form of this character. He will probably find one age at which the character seems most comfortable. However, he must attempt to experience as many stages of this person's life as class time allows. New circumstances and activities should be sought daily. A whole human being is being formed, and the actor will want to experience as much of this person's life as possible.

Meeting People

For the first time in the work, relationships with other people are encouraged. Free time should be extended so that actor's can work with others. Each individual should begin alone until the desire to reach other people becomes interesting or necessary. The actor should be cautioned to stay with people only as long as his interest is sustained. Communication should occur without using verbalization or "sign" language. The actor must speak with his body. The following three exercises are designed to explore "public" behavior. Each exercise will occur in a different location. The actors must choose a set of conditions before entering the environment.

The following instructions are to be repeated for each of the exercises in this section:

1. *Do not think about playing a character*, or you will trap yourself into a stereotype.

2. Answer the following questions, and from the answers you will know who you are and how old you are:

Where are you coming from? Where are you going? Why? What do you want to do while you wait? What (imaginary) objects are you carrying with you (e.g., newspapers, suitcases, purses)?

3. As you proceed in each exercise, you will notice a "center" from which your physical actions will stem. Make your customary inventory of your whole body.

Meeting People
"I spent most of my time watching other people. When they thought I was the criminal, they all looked at me at once. The feeling was overwhelming. I could feel it in every part of my body."

4. Do not spend any time worrying over making these decisions. Make impulsive choices and proceed from there.
5. Use these exercises to discover how you react under pressures with other people.
6. Keep yourself open to how each new relationship will affect you.

OBSERVATION
The student will find, upon later examination of his journal, that his choices probably came from prior observations of himself in the mask and from a compilation of his emotional experiences in free time and Discovery exercises. Remember, the more open the student can be, the fewer limitations he will put on his creative sources.

Step 34: Waiting for a Bus

TIME
Forty-five minutes.

PURPOSE
To learn about yourself through encounters with others; to react to a frustrating inconvenient situation while in the company of strangers.

PROCESS
The instructor sets up the following environment using rehearsal furniture and props: Build a play space which is small and confined by four "walls." Make an entrance into the Waiting Room from outside and an exit to the Arrival/Departure area for the buses. Use a bench that can seat three people and two or three side chairs. Provide areas for coffee and candy concession machines, for a telephone booth, and for a door leading to rest rooms. Instructions for the actors:
1. You will be entering the bus terminal.
2 Ask the questions: Where are you coming from? Where are you going? Why? What do you want to do while you wait? What objects are you carrying with you?
3. Now, enter the terminal at your own pace.
4. Everyone in the terminal is a stranger to you.
5. Allow connections with people to occur naturally and honestly out of the situation.
6. Do not force communication.

7. Sustain yourself without talking because you choose not to speak. You may use sound.
8. This is the last bus leaving for your destination.
9. Wait for the bus.
10. Do not pretend to wait.
11. Do not show what it means to wait. Really wait.

SIDE COACHING

Voice as if from a loudspeaker: "Ladies and gentlemen, I regret to inform you, but the bus has been unavoidably detained."

Loudspeaker: "The weather seems to be getting very bad. There is a serious snow heading in this direction and road conditions are not good."

The telephone is out of order.

The concession machine is out of order.

The thermostat is broken and the air feels stuffy.

The temperature in the room has dropped considerably, and now it is very cold.

(Instructor walks into the environment and removes a chair.)

Loudspeaker: "We are doing our best to get the bus here, ladies and gentlemen, but unfortunately the road conditions are getting worse."

(Instructor removes two more chairs.)

The toilets are out of order.

The room is icy cold.

Loudspeaker: "We do not think there will be another bus tonight."

Loudspeaker: "There seems to be a bus coming, but it can only hold five or six passengers. Those people who absolutely must leave the terminal tonight, please line up."

Loudspeaker: "The bus is much too overcrowded. We can only take three people."

Loudspeaker: "We deeply regret the inconvenience, ladies and gentlemen."

NOTE

After the exercise, instruct the actors to return to their journals and write their response to this experience.

Step 35: Riding a Subway Train

TIME

Forty-five minutes.

PURPOSE

To learn about yourself through new encounters; to deal with frightening, unpleasant conditions while in the company of others.

PROCESS

The instructor sets up the following environment for the actors:
Provide an area for a subway car that is narrow and not too long, forcing people to crowd together. Place six or eight chairs in pairs for the train. There should be fewer seats than are necessary for the group, causing greater discomfort in the space. Indicate a waiting platform on which to stand before the train arrives. Indicate another narrow, small area on to which the passengers will have to file in the middle of the exercise. Instructions to the actors:

1. You are waiting on a subway platform for a train.
2. You are total strangers. No verbal communication.
3. Give yourselves entirely new circumstances: Where are you coming from? Where are you going? Why? What do you want to do while you wait? What objects are you carrying with you?
4. When you are ready, walk in and wait for the train.

SIDE COACHING

Train coming. Hear the sound. See the light. Train rushes past you.
Train coming. Hear the sound. See the light. Train rushes past you.
Train coming. Hear the sound. See the light. Train stops.
Doors start to open. Close quickly. Train lurches forward slightly. Stops.
Doors open.
Train doors close. Train lurches forward and continues on.
Train veers abruptly to the left.
Train veers abruptly to the right.
Another train roars by on the left.
Train stops. Lurches forward. Stops. Lurches forward and continues.
Train veers to the left. Train veers to the right.
Lights go out. Lights on. Lights out.
Train stops. Starts abruptly. Stops. (Light still out.)
Train starts. Goes a few feet. Stops. Lights go on.
Train stops abruptly. (Lights still out.)
Train starts. Goes a few feet. Stops. Lights go on.
Train stops abruptly.
Loudspeaker: "Ladies and gentlemen . . ." (muffle voice so it is inaudible).
Train lurches forward. Stops.
Loudspeaker: "Ladies . . ." (muffled).

Loudspeaker: "Ladies and gentlemen, we are having severe electrical problems with this train. We will have to get off it before we reach the next station. We are sorry for the blackout, but we are temporarily out of light. When the doors open, please move out of the train very carefully on to the planking that has been set up for you. Be alert to the dangerous third rail. Stay on the planks. Watch your step."
Train passes by. It remains dark.
Next train arrives. Slowly, carefully, go back on the train the same route you used coming off.
New train starts up. Stops. Lights flash out. Lights go on.
Train moves forward.
Loudspeaker: "Ladies and gentlemen, we have just received word that there is a dangerous criminal on your train. We will have police guards at the next station. When we have more details we will let you know."
Train stops. Train lurches forward and moves on.
Loudspeaker: "The person is wearing something black. Be very careful, this person is armed and dangerous."
Train veers to the right.
Loudspeaker: "This person is wearing—(choose someone with something distinctive on who is in the center of the crowd.) There will be a reward for helping the police in the capture of this criminal."
Lights go out. Train veers to the left. Lights go on.
Train pulls into the station.
Return to your journals and write your responses to this exercise.

Step 36: Attending a Reception Honoring the President of the United States

TIME
Forty-five minutes.

PURPOSE
To learn about yourself through encounters with others; to experience a relatively trouble-free, pleasant social situation with others.

PROCESS
Instructor sets up following situation: Arrange a few chairs around a large open space. Indicate an entrance to the room and a bar area. Instructions for the actors:

1. You have been invited to a reception honoring the president of the United States.
2. Give yourself entirely new circumstances: Where? What? Why?
3. Prepare yourself to attend the reception.
4. Come alone.
5. No verbal communication.
6. Enter when you are ready.

SIDE COACHING
Loudspeaker: "Ladies and gentlemen, music for your dancing pleasure, a waltz." (Instructor should change the type of dance music periodically.)
Loudspeaker: "Ladies and gentlemen, we are sorry the president has been delayed. Please enjoy the music and the refreshments. We will inform you as soon as his motorcade arrives."
Loudspeaker: "We have received word that the president is on his way here. Please be ready to greet him."
"Ladies and gentlemen, the president of the United States has been shot."
Leave the reception and go to your journals.

OBSERVATION
The public situations in the preceding exercises have given the actor the opportunity to remove the usual social limitations from his behavior and imagination. Under extreme pressure, the actor has discovered that he is permitted to use his immediate emotional responses. Nothing prevents the feelings from surfacing; there are far fewer social barriers within the structure of these explorations than in the "real world." Feelings can now float up to the surface of cognizance and permeate the actor. After anger and frustration have been played out, and the actor is conscious of the special joy in using emotions to the fullest, there is an active search to permit other feelings. In addition, since interaction is encouraged, there is now a place to test out these new discoveries.

Finding What Suits You

The atmosphere in the classroom is filled with the need to "try things." Actors are ready to face the challenge of new stimuli. They want to test out their feelings, find out more about themselves and their emerging characters. Although they are not yet conscious of it, things are beginning to come together for them and will soon be definable.

Finding What Suits You
"I attacked the clothing like a kid going crazy. I wanted to put everything on at once. I went to all the male things first. Then I really wanted to try the female things—a whole new experience with those things. More and more fantasies running wild—Hats!"

The next two exercises provide rich possibilities for learning more about oneself and the mask. Actors invariably attack them with unbridled energy and excitement. Clothing will be used from this point on in the course work. However, it is best not to start free time with the clothes. The actors should be alone for a while each day, in their neutral leotards and tights, to allow something to open up inside them before they choose what they want to wear.

Step 37: Trying on Clothes

TIME
Entire class session (ninety to one hundred and twenty minutes).

PURPOSE
To release all feelings and play freely with many different colors and styles of clothing; to discover new centers and behavioral patterns through dressing up.

PROCESS
No instructions are given in this session. After ten minutes of private free time, the large amounts of clothing that have been accumulated for to-day's exercise are set out. After the first moments of tentative handling, with eyes sending the appeal "Am I allowed?," the actors will know exactly what they want to do with the clothing. The group should use the clothes without any restrictions for the whole session. Results from the exploration should be carefully noted in the journals.

OBSERVATION
Dressing up in fanciful and sometimes forbidden clothing is something most people did when they were children. There was innocent, whole-hearted pleasure attached to dressing like a king or queen or looking like father or mother. These playful, delightful pleasures are rekindled for the actor. The clothing grants permission to freely experiment and play. In this exercise, shirts may be turned into pants, and capes into skirts and headdresses. Since there are no rules or instructions provided, fanciful handling of the pieces is explored in imaginative ways. People are very possessive with some clothing. They have been working for themselves for such a long time that sharing feels like a tremendous deprivation. Sometimes they will go to great lengths to get back an article that some-

one else is using. The amazing thing about working with the clothing is that the actors have an instant intuition about what is right for them. Actually, this intuition is based upon the last six or seven weeks of building and storing a foundation for the character. Suddenly the clothing affords definitions; it provides a coming together of feelings. The group should use the clothes without any restrictions for the whole sessions. Results from the exploration should be carefully noted in the journals. On the second day when the clothes have been put out, actors should be encouraged to try things they have not touched before. Even if the clothing looks or feels instantly wrong, it should be experienced. The actor never knows before he tries something what it can do to him. If nothing else profitable occurs from the "wrong" clothing, at least he can be assured that he knows what is "right."

Step 38: Exploring Language

TIME
Thirty minutes.

PURPOSE
To introduce extensive vocal exploration of words and phrases; to have the words serve as a stimulus that allows immediate impulses and ideas to be explored.

PROCESS
After the group has settled on clothing that feels right, call out a list of words and phrases. Each one is to be vocally explored for its multiple possibilities of melody, pitch, intensity, meaning, etc. A physical statement should be sought to underscore each verbalization (see Step 30 "Making Your Body Speak," in the "Discovery" section). Then the actor should take these verbal and physical statements to one another and interrelate. Instruct the actor to repeat, explore, and respond to the words immediately as he hears them. Bodies must be open and ready to receive the words as they are called out. Sample words:

Go	Flowers
Nasty	Sexy
Shit	I'm having fun
Warm pudding	Sing a song for me
Mysterious	Pain in the ass
Delicate	Come

SIDE COACHING

Work alone.

Work for yourself.

Fill your body with the sound.

Work from you first impulse to find meaning. Continue to search for meanings: abstract and concrete ones.

Don't drop your body. Keep it vitalized as you explore sound. Clarify the physical and vocal statements.

Take your word to other people and explore a relationship for a moment or two. When it yields you a discovery, move on to your own space or into someone else's. Do not stay with anyone longer than you need to.

**BRIDGING THE LAST EXERCISE
INTO THE NEXT ONE**

Words and phrases should be added to the end portion of free time for the next two class sessions, as they will be used for the next exercise.

Recognizing Needs and Desires

At this point in the work, though the actor is not necessarily aware of the character's personality, he is usually conscious of certain consistent behavior patterns. These are the *constants* that the actor has been alerted to look for from the earliest sessions. While the instructor should continue to encourage finding and exploring new centers, the actor must develop a sense of what "fits" and trust what is full and organic. Certain feelings and moods will seem undeniable. Now that clothing and some use of language have been added to aid in the adventure of developing the character, more controlled and purposeful exposure to other individuals is necessary. The following exercises will help the actor identify and determine some of the basic motivations, needs, and desires for the character.

Step 39: Finding Yourself in a Place with Someone

TIME

Fifteen to thirty minutes for each improvisation.

PURPOSE

To discover and explore your motivations and behavior within circumstances that evolve from a specific relationshp in a specific environment;

Recognizing Needs and Desires
*"I must follow through with stronger intentions—know how I feel
and then act upon it."*

to repeat the situation that evolved from the improvisation and put it into
an economical form.

PROCESS
Pair off the group in twos, assign them a space in the room, and identify a
specific environment for each couple. All the couples work in the room
simultaneously and at their own pace. Sample environments: bathroom,
bedroom, park bench, living room, lunch counter, elevator, jail cell, attic,
cellar. Instructions for the actor:
1. Decide why you are in this place together.
2. Do not communicate with one another verbally.
3. At some appropriate moment felt by each one of you, one word or
   phrase taken from the free time words and phrases, may be spoken
   once.

4. As you do the improvisation, you will find an overall intention with accompanying conflicts and obstacles.
5. When you both sense a natural ending has been reached, lift the masks and briefly discuss what has occurred.
6. Put the masks back on and repeat the scene.
7. This time get to the main conflict or crisis sooner and clean away any excess activity.
8. The final improvisation should be simple, clear, and short with a logical beginning, middle, and end.
9. After the second time through the scene, return to your journals and answer the questions in the student's section.
10. If desired, you may change your clothes for the next improvisation.

OBSERVATION
Two class sessions should be utilized for these improvisations. The more partners and environments with which each actor can work, the more numerous the opportunities for discovery. At first the students may feel a need to create something dramatic rather than let the situation organically evolve. However, with repetition of the exercise and a variety of partners and places, there is less fear and worry about producing a performance. Each actor uses the situation to experiment and explore. He does the scene a second time in order to clarify the form, economize on the actions, and firm the decisions made the first time.

Step 40: Receiving a Surprise Call

TIME
Fifteen minutes.

PURPOSE
To permit the actor to begin to realize who the character (the Mask) is; to respond to someone intimately involved in the character's past life; to find the voice and the words of the character.

PROCESS
Instructions for the actors:
1. Take a chair into a private space.
2. When you are comfortable, you (the Mask) will receive a phone call from someone you have not spoken to in at least three years. This

should not be someone from the actor's real life. This will be someone who was close to you in the past.

3. Start to fill that person in on what you have been doing during that time. You may speak freely, letting the vocal pattern, rhythm, and words organically spring from you.
4. Do not stay seated during the whole conversation.
5. Use your space completely.
6. Do not plan before hand who will be calling.
7. Answer the phone and discover who is on the other end.
8. If the caller asks you questions you cannot answer at this time, respond truthfully by saying you do not know.
9. After the conversation has been established, the person on the other end will put pressure on you in some way. Respond as best as you can.
10. When you hang up, lift the mask, go to your journal, and write down what you discovered about this character's life.

Step 41: Calling to Get a Job

TIME
Fifteen minutes.

PURPOSE
To learn some facts about the character's present circumstances; to explore responding to a stranger (the possible employer).

PROCESS
The following instructions are given to the actors:
1. Make no prior decisions.
2. Take a chair to a space.
3. When you are ready, pick up a phone and call someone about a job that you saw advertised.
4. Do not make an appointment to have an interview. Instead, sell yourself on the telephone and try to get the job right then and there.
5. During the conversation, the prospective employer will put great pressure on you.
6. Respond as best you can.
7. Finish at your own pace.
8. Return to your journal and write down what you discovered in this encounter.

Solidifying the Character/Making Decisions
*"My characteristics suddenly seem consistent to me. What I believed
were totally different characters were really different moods of one
person."*

Solidifying the Character/Making Decisions

After so many explanatory and improvisatory sessions, working from different centers, and having varied objectives for each exercise, the idea of solidifying and making decisions for one character may seem frightening and perhaps impossible. The actor may feel he has already played a hundred characters; how can he choose one? Prior discussion has pointed out that in spite of this state of confusion the actor has indeed been building emotional and behavioral patterns that will soon be expressed in a singular personality. The previous two exercises—"Receiving a Surprise Call" and "Calling to Get a Job"—have caused the character to begin to find a form. Fragments or pieces of the personality are emerging. Some facts about the character's life are now known. What the actor now needs is an exercise to help put all the pieces together—a catalyst to bring the character into the actor's consciousness.

Step 42: Getting Interviewed

TIME
Fifteen minutes for each actor.

PURPOSE
To find the character; to solidify the physical and psychological center of the character; to discover facts about the character's past and present life.

PROCESS
Each character will now be interviewed by the rest of the group. Place one chair or bench in front of the class. Each interview takes at least fifteen minutes and every person in the group must be interviewed before going on with any new exercises. Only the character being interviewed will wear a mask. For the first time each Mask will face a large group of unmasked people who will ask him the questions. The following instructions are given to the actor:
1. This is an extraordinary opportunity to discover who you are.
2. Do not plan any answers before you are interviewed.
3. While you are unmasked and listening to others being interviewed, avoid the temptation to anticipate answers or make comparisons to your own character.

4. Take the risk and allow all the responses to come out of the moment.
5. If you do not know the answer to any question, say that you can't answer that at this time.
6. The questions are not intended to trap the character. There is no pressure to know all the answers.
7. The questions are asked solely to aid you in making discoveries about the character's past history, present status, personal tastes, inner longings, private fears, needs, and preoccupations.
8. The interview begins the search for those things that are pertinent to the character's life.
9. The character's name will be requested. If one comes off your tongue, just let it happen. Later you may want to change it, but do not be afraid to commit yourself to a name now.
10. Walk over to the chair and introduce yourself.
11. Do not stay seated during the entire interview.
12. Allow your feelings to go through your whole body as you answer questions.
13. After the interview, record your discoveries in your journal with the aid of the questions in the Actor's Guide.

Sample questions for interview:
1. What is your name?
2. Where do you come from?
3. Where are we now?
4. What year is this?
5. Who do you live with?
6. Do you work?
7. What do you enjoy doing with your time?
8. What do you find most attractive about yourself? Most interesting? Most unappealing?
9. What do you hate to do?
10. What are your close friends like?
11. Why did you choose what you are wearing?
12. Do you have any special talents?
13. Can you do something for us (sing, dance, tell a story, etc.)?
14. If you could go anywhere in the world, where would it be?
15. If you had your wish to have anything, what would it be?
16. What bothers you about other people?
17. Can you tell us about a particularly happy time in your life? A sad time?
18. What books do you like? Music? Food?

OBSERVATION

For the rest of the group, none of the information learned about the other characters during their interviews is usable. Thus, when they meet each other in free time or in a class exercise, they must always encounter one another as if for the first time. This is helpful for continually making new discoveries from other relationships. In addition, it will give each character the opportunity to grow and change, not to be boxed in by anyone else's expectations. Everything that has formed the basic foundation of this character has come out of a combination of the actor's own inner instincts and impulses and the intense study of the mask. The character is made up of similar personality traits to the actor. This is unavoidable because the character comes from *inside* the actor. The difference between the actor and the Mask is the direction that those traits take; the character feels and does things very differently from the actor. The strong, emotional explorations that have preceded the character's development have opened the actor to powerful feelings. These feelings, coupled with the size and strength of the mask's form and the full body commitment to each action, have produced a character that is larger than life.

The next part of the work—perhaps the most fulfilling period of all—is to actively search out all the levels of personality. For the first time outside of class, in homework assignments, the actors will start to make conscious decisions for the character. Reentering the class and putting the mask on again, the actor will be transformed into the character and will immediately know if the decisions were correct. The character is alive now and will answer for himself. Because this character is completely the actor's own creation, it would be wise to talk about him as separate from the actor, to refer to the character in the third person, as "he" and "she."

Extension: Layering and Broadening the Character

Extension: Layering and Broadening the Character
"She is all talk and no action. She latches on to every available man but backs off when sex is mentioned. Something happened to her when she was young that made her inhibited yet still vain. I must find out what it was."

The actor now knows who this Mask is; some of the basic psychology is clear, the physical center is located and the body organized accordingly, the voice and language patterns have been identified. Most probably the character has a name (if not, it will be shortly forthcoming), and there are many facts already determined in regard to the character's history and present life-style. It is time now to pose a myriad of questions that when answered will fill in and broaden the character's being. Some of these answers will be found in free time relationships and other spontaneous encounters. Others will come from the planning and preparing of homework assignments for later presentation in class. As with the work of the past eight weeks, all the decisions will be tested by direct experiences in the class sessions.

The exercises described in this chapter are very useful in probing and extending the Mask. However, the actor must take the responsibility to make other discoveries in the amount of time still available. After all, only the individual actor is aware of how much he already knows and understands about the character. Thus, he must take it upon himself to explore the remaining unknown territories. Sometimes he will have to give himself definite goals for free time instead of just letting it "happen." The actor must continually ask himself:

1. What is left?
2. What don't I know?
3. What situations can I set up that will tell me more?
4. Who can I tap that I haven't yet worked with?
5. What objectives can I give myself that will put the character under greater stress or give him more pleasure?
6. What was the character like at age eighteen?
7. What will he be like at age seventy?
8. What would happen if. . . ?

In other words, what does it take to truly be another human being?

Building the World of the Character

It is time for the actor to discover and determine the particular way in which the character lives: the wardrobe, the home environment, the personal belongings, the job, the hobbies, and the habits. For every future class session, the character should be dressed appropriately for that day's activity. While the actor may use any of the class's store of costumes, he will probably need to find many other outside sources of clothing. A great deal of thought must go into every detail of the character's attire. The Mask will need shoes, underwear, wraps, hats, jewelry, etc. It would be a mistake for the actor to use his own favorite clothing and accessories for the character; they probably will not *feel right* once they are on the character. The actor will have to try things for awhile before the true taste of the character is determined. In fact, it is wise to keep as open as possible in case an unexpected item brings out an unknown personality trait in the character. There may be several discards, but it will not take long before the actor will have the ability to make instant and appropri-

Building the World of the Character
"When she was alone, I found that she was boxed in. She wanted to be around people. She doesn't like being alone and not too many things hold her interest."

ate choices. Thrift shops and friends' closets can be valuable sources for building a wardrobe.

The characters should dress themselves each day, instead of the actor dressing before the class begins. After the warm-up, when the masks are on, the character can determine how he wants to look. Combing and styling hair are also a part of the daily routine. Arranging and choosing clothing follow the "toilette." When the character handles it, a cheap polyester shirt, chosen by chance by an actor, can become a sensuous, silken dream. A modest, shy actor could be a flamboyant character who is an exhibitionist when dressing. In other words, valuable behavior can be determined with the preparations to start the day's activity.

Step 43: Keeping Busy at Home Alone

TIME
Entire class session (ninety to one hundred and twenty minutes).

PURPOSE
To explore the character's private world; to find out what activities and objects fill the character's life; to discover how the character reacts when left to his own resources.

HOMEWORK
Bring a shopping bag filled with objects which you believe will interest your character. Choose a large number of things, because you will be working with them for two hours. In addition, bring some items that help to create a private environment for the character, a place where he or she lives. Have the character dress for an evening at home.

PROCESS
Instructions for the actors:
1. The character is at home for the evening.
2. Decorate the space to individual taste and keep busy doing personal chores.
3. Do not plan in advance how the character will handle the chores or the objects, or how much time will be spent with any one thing. Discover this with the doing.
4. The character is completely alone, and the area is totally private.
5. Use this as an opportunity to discover the most personal behavior.

OBSERVATIONS

There are interesting results from this exercise. Most often, people barricade themselves within their own areas by using objects which make the boundaries. Blankets cover chairs to form tents, benches are set up to make walls. People like privacy—not an uncommon desire among human beings. Chores often include reading special magazines, putting on makeup, playing cards, shaving, clipping coupons from newspapers, washing and setting hair, dusting and polishing objects, listening to music, and most surprising, praying. No one is inactive. Even if the character is resting for a moment, one can sense that it is a "purposeful" rest; the actor is not dropping out. Characters hum or talk to themselves while they work. (There is a strong sensation for the instructor, who remains a silent observer for two hours, that the instructor is something of a voyeur, looking in on other people's private lives.)

Step 44: Keeping a Conflict Hidden

TIME

Entire class session (ninety to one hundred and twenty minutes).

PURPOSE

To continue to build the world of the character; to help the actor explore the character's behavior when he is hiding his real thoughts from others; to help to develop subtext; to continue the exploration of expressing thoughts and ideas without words.

PROCESS

Pair off the group into couples by determining which people should work together. Characters that have conflicting life-styles and needs should be placed together. For each partner create improvisational situations and environments with motivations that will put the two persons in strong conflict with one another. These motivations, or objectives, should remain hidden from the other partner as long as possible during the first work-through of the improvisation. Examples:

1. Place: Dinner at an elegant restaurant.
   Objectives: Male—I want to hurry with dinner and take her home with me and seduce her. Female—I have come with him only as an "admission ticket" to this place, so that I may be seen by the best people and catch the eye of the person I am really attracted to.
   Clothing: very dressy.

2. Place: Person A's home
   Objectives: A—I must get dressed and get to a job interview before it is too late; B—I must sell you this, or I will lose my job.
   Clothing: A—pajamas; B—nice street clothes.
3. Place: A's apartment
   Objectives: Female—I want him to make love to me before the others arrive. Male—I want to check out this place for robbery.
   Clothing: Very dressy.
4. Place: A sports field or arena.
   Objectives: A—the man from the Olympics is secretly here and watching my form. I must make a terrific impression on him by beating B. B—I want to instruct A on the fine points of this game since A is such a clod.
   Clothing: Sports clothing or whatever your character likes to play. (The actors will work out the details of what game to play when they are together. They might even want to invent a game for themselves.)
5. Place: Waiting room of an office.
   Objectives: A—I want to find out if B is waiting for an interview for the same job as I am. B—Same as A.
   Clothing: Nice daytime clothes. Since the first working of the exercise will be improvised, do not tell the actors what they will be involved in during the next class session. Simply inform them to bring in clothing that will be appropriate for their characters for an assigned time of day or occasion. The following instructions are given to the actors:
1. You will be given a situation and an objective.
2. Your character will justify the objective by filling in whatever background and specifics you need.
3. You must do everything possible to keep your real motives hidden and at the same time try to win your objective.
4. These situations will be worked on simultaneously with the whole class three times. There will be a different goal for each work-through:
   a. Discovery: To find the relationship between the partners and the character's justification of the objectives.
   b. Economy: To hone down and clean away excess and develop the situation with a beginning, middle, and end.
   c. Filling the Body: To do the entire situation nonverbally, finding a way to communicate without pantomime. (not speaking to one another becomes the *choice* of the characters.) Note: This last work-through will probably change the course of the action. This is certainly permissible. It will also sharpen the events of the scene, make the actor concentrate on an active, succinct subtext, and force a more interesting, committed use of the body to communicate the

whole situation. After the third time, the nonverbal version will be shown to the rest of the class.

SPECIAL NOTE

The preceding exercises and the ones to follow are all individually shown to the class (except for the special group events: the party and the outing). Masks should be lifted while watching others so that the actors can be objective observers and offer suggestions to other students. While the major emphasis in the work is still on building the characters, and certainly each character's motivations are never evaluated or questioned, the actors must realize that in this portion of the work, their ability to articulate and communicate ideas must be tested and perfected. *The outer form is now as important as the inner impulse.*

Step 45: Speaking about Personal Matters on the Telephone

TIME

As many class sessions as are needed to see all the exercises individually. There should also be after-class commentary and further rehearsal in free time. Then one more session to rerun all the exercises.

PURPOSE

To explore new facets of the Mask's private life and personality; to put the discoveries into an interesting set of circumstances which can be easily understood and appreciated by an audience; to shape the piece.

HOMEWORK

At home, develop a three-to-five-minute set of circumstances for your character in which, at least part of the time, he or she will be talking to someone on the phone. The nature of the phone call should be personal, and the content should reveal something to you hitherto unexplored or unknown. Choose a place (private or public) for the call. Create the environment with whatever objects are needed and use your imagination to fill in the rest of the walls and furniture. The piece must have a clear beginning, middle, and end. Your character should be involved in another task or activity before or during the call, which will help to reveal real feelings through behavior. If you wish, use free time in class to rehearse.

PROCESS

Instructions for the actors: When your mask is on, you will probably find that some of what you planned will need to be changed. Permit yourself to respond to these changes easily. Create the reality and listen to the person on the other end of the phone. At the end of your piece, lift your mask, and we will discuss it. When all the pieces are completed, they will be shown again without discussion. The second showing will give you an opportunity to use people's suggestions and clean the piece up further. It will also help you re-create the event and make it happen as if for the first time.

OBSERVATIONS

The results of this exercise are always very exciting. The characters are invariably freer than the actors by now, and the pieces show great imagination along with totally truthful, organic extensions of the personalities that we see developing. Some examples that have occurred in past classes:

1. A pathetically shy, but extremely polite and cautious, young man dialed several numbers at random to make obscene and violent phone calls to pour out the rage he felt at finding his personal things tampered with. In spite of his extreme frustration, and the obscene content of the call, he was neatly folding his laundry.

2. A lonely, awkward, ugly girl was dancing and cavorting with great delight as she dressed for her first date. During one of her more robust sexual fantasies, the young man called and canceled the date.

3. An arrogant, self-willed young lady who always got her own way sneaked into the orphanage office and desperately tried to call people to beg them to adopt her.

4. An old derelict, once a Spanish nobleman, was forced at gunpoint to make an obscene call to a young girl. As the call progressed, he realized that the girl was enjoying it, and his own reactions were violently jumping between fear, embarrassment, and excitement.

SPECIAL NOTE

Perhaps it would be well to offer a precaution about the discussions that take place after each piece is shown for the first time. Every attempt should be made *not* to tell the actor how to solve the problems with the piece or how to execute it. In mask work, the best way to keep the actor's imagination stimulated and alive is to require him to solve the problem himself. The most helpful comment you can offer an actor is, "Find another way. That way is not working." Most of the time, the solution to the problem will be a simple one if the actor will relax and *let the character find it.* If the actor is being entirely honest with the character, the character will be able to take complete responsibility for his own actions.

Extending the Boundaries of the World of the Character

The world of the character needs expanding, not just within the mind and imagination of the actor but through practical experience in the class sessions. Even though the actors have been cautioned to meet each other anew every time they enter the room, eventually the relationships do become predictable. The characters tend to seek the same alliances day after day. They know with whom they can feel safe and enjoy themselves. They know who their adversaries are. You can tell yourself that you do not know anything about the next person, but after weeks of interacting, each time you see him your reactions will usually be the same. Thus, new situations must be introduced for further development. In addition, the actor is hungering for new events. The actor is fully aware of the magical power he has with this character. All he has to do is put on the mask and his body and mind will literally transform him so that he *becomes* the character. Therefore, the desire to be challenged by new circumstances is strong. The actor wants to let the character react to and make all his own decisions.

Vistors to the class are an excellent source of new responses. The characters know instantly what to do and what to say to a stranger. The character's response to a visitor might be totally opposite to what that actor behind the mask would do. It is exciting to experience the openness and truthfulness of this behavior. It might prove embarrassing as well, as what once happened when a rather quiet, withdrawn student donned her mask and tried to flirt with a professor who was watching the class. He resisted, and she lambasted him for his retreat. When she saw the professor later in the day, she felt compelled to apologize and say it was the character, not she, who was making the advances.

The next series of exercises are designed to open the world of the character even more, and to strengthen the actor's confidence in the character's ability to function anywhere, anytime, and in any way.

Extending the Boundaries of the World of the Character
"The premise for my piece was right but each beat has to be stronger, with more contrast in the whole thing. I must explore her façade—the image that she is trying to create on the outside—not what she is really thinking."

Step 46: Going to a Party

TIME
Entire class session (ninety to one hundred and twenty minutes)

PURPOSE
To discover personality and behavior from social circumstances.

PROCESS
Ask two or three unlikely leaders to organize a party for the group. Every character should be responsible for some contribution to the activity. Some might bring the food, others the decorations, while others provide the entertainment. Each character should come dressed in his best clothes. The entire affair must be coordinated and executed by the characters, *not* the actors. The whole session is given over to the party. Real music for dancing should be provided. Visitors to the group are welcome.

OBSERVATION
How the character behaves under the pressure of a social atmosphere can be very revealing. Sometimes surprising friendships develop, and unknown fears about popularity and belonging are stirred and brought forward. On one occasion, a photographer was invited, and she added to the fun by taking "prom" portraits.

SPECIAL NOTE
The next two exercises test the character's reactions to the stress and frustration brought on by absurd and malfunctioning objects in the character's own world. The first, "Getting Stuck," is an improvised group exercise administered by the instructor. It is really a preparation for the more complicated and carefully planned second exercise, "Getting Into Trouble." It directly relates back to the early sensory exercises from the "Discovery" section: "Pumping Water from a Well" (Step 11), "Hanging Pictures on a Wall" (Step 13), "Doing a Private Task" (Step 26). This time, however, the conditions and circumstances are filled in by the characters: Where are they? What are they doing? Why are they doing it? In this way, the physical and mental means to solve the problems will be the characters' not the actors' choices.

Step 47: Getting Stuck

TIME
Thirty to forty-five minutes.

PURPOSE
To explore behavior in frustrating circumstances; to elicit purposeful and logical behavior when dealing with the illogical circumstances; to discover comic potential in solving extreme problems.

HOMEWORK
Bring clothes for a workday around the character's home.

PROCESS
Instructions for the actors:
1. Find your own space.
2. You are alone at home.
3. Begin a chore that you have been meaning to do—fixing the sink, planting new flowers, repainting a room, etc.
4. Have a set of appropriate tools with which to work by your side.
5. Plan for a long session to get this job done.
6. Now, get involved in the task.

SIDE COACHING
(After at least five to ten minutes of concentrated, silent work.)
As you are working, some part of your body gets stuck. Maybe your foot is caught, or your rear end gets glued, or one arm is pinned. Find the part of you that is stuck and try to free it. Pull and push in every way you can. Unfortunately, you can't seem to get yourself free. Try to use one of the tools that you have been working with to pry yourself free. It may be a little awkward to manipulate it, but try your best.
Try changing your body position to exert more pressure on the stuck part to get it out.
Try another position with another tool if you have one.
Ooops, another part of your body is stuck. Try to work your way out of this ridiculous situation—two parts of you stuck.
Use another tool, even if it means you have to manipulate it under your chin or between your legs or with your toes.
Someone is watching you. Try to continue your original task in spite of your stuck parts. Convince the person by your action that what you are doing is normal and intentional.

While realigning your body to hide from the person's eyes, another part of you gets stuck. Now there are three parts stuck. Try to maintain your dignity in spite of the terrible situation.

I don't know if it is possible to hide your predicament anymore. Maybe you need to address yourself to finding a solution to your problem. Get the stuck parts free. Use any means you can. Try every possible body contortion plus help from any of the tools.

Try some more ways. Don't rest. The person is watching you, but you must get free. Don't leave any means untouched, no matter how useless or silly they may seem at first.

Oh, here comes one part free. Freedom for one, two to go! Now go at the problem with renewed vigor. Find a solution.

Step 48: Getting into Trouble

TIME
As many class sessions as needed to see all the exercises individually. After class commentary and further rehearsal in free time are utilized, the exercises are then repeated for one more session.

PURPOSE
To explore a new facet of personality and behavior; to find the obstacles that cause the greatest indignity and/or frustration; to put discoveries into an interesting set of circumstances which can be easily understood and appreciated by an audience; to shape the piece.

HOMEWORK
At home, develop a three-to-five-minute silent piece in which the character is at odds with something which gets him into trouble, and from which he must find a solution. The situation should cause your character the greatest possible indignity. Try to use objects and environmental conditions as the major obstacles. Remember, silence is from choice, thus, there should be no pantomiming of language. Use this as an opportunity to uncover another layer of the character's personality, hitherto unseen. Have a clear beginning, middle, and end.

OBSERVATIONS
Along with the revelations of personality and the continuing exploration of fullness, simplicity, economy, and clarity of nonverbal communication, these two exercises (Steps 47 and 48) can help the actor develop a

comic use of self from completely realistic and honest circumstances. The character is truly enmeshed in a problem that challenges his resourcefulness and threatens his dignity. In order to find a solution to the troublesome situation, the character may have to rely on absurd means, utilize incongruous objects to accomplish the goal and "save face." For example, if you are on your way to a dinner in which you are the guest of honor, and you step in dog's leavings and try to scrape it off, and it gets on your suit, and the only thing with which you have to wipe it off your suit is your tie . . . well, that is the idea of what it means to pit oneself against an obstacle while trying to maintain one's self-esteem. An added benefit of working on comic technique in these exercises is the elimination of mugging. Mugging is using your face to "indicate" thoughts and predicament. When you wear a mask, all that you have with which to communicate is your body. *Nothing will read in your face.* Some past exercises have been:

1. In a public park, a down-and-out bum, who was trying to hang on to his last shreds of self-esteem, had to use the toilet, but the bathrooms were filled. While waiting outside the door, a bee began to plague him. He soon became involved in the pursuit of the bee, and he forgot about his bursting bowels and "let go" during the chase.

2. A desperately shy, frightened woman was having lunch at a restaurant lunch counter—an event that was overwhelming in itself. She was so nervous about being watched while she ate that she played with a soda bottle to relieve her tension. When she was ready to leave, she found her finger was stuck in the bottle. She had to find a way to pay her check, "steal" the attached bottle, and leave the place unnoticed.

3. A cocky, incorrigible, pregnant teenager visited an art museum for the first time in her life. She was delighted with everything she saw, and she tried to pose herself as the characters in the paintings and sculptures. After making a fetching Botticelli *Primavera*, she came upon Michelangelo's *David*. She was irresistably attracted to it, and while touching it she found that the penis came off in her hands. She could not get it back on no matter how hard she tried. Finally she had to leave it in the middle of the room, in the hope that it would be mistaken for another precious work of art.

Step 49: Going on an Outing

TIME

Entire class session (ninety to one hundred and twenty minutes)

PURPOSE
To reveal the outside world to the character; to test his behavior to new people and places.

HOMEWORK
Bring clothes to wear for taking a walk outside.

PROCESS
The group will go for a walk in the neighborhood. Window shop, stop in stores, talk to people along the way. Give the Mask every possible opportunity to explore his reactions to all of the sensory stimuli of the environment and the people he meets.

OBSERVATION
If ever the principle of safety behind the mask is tested, this is the occasion. In the "real world," the actor learns that he must trust the character he has so painstakingly built. Given a free rein, the character will react accordingly to his individual needs and view of the world. The actor will return from the trip feeling exhilarated because of the sense of freedom and accomplishment. In an unprotected environment (the classroom is very safe and comfortable) the character's behavior will solidify. The actor will have indisputable evidence of the realness and effectiveness of the creation. All of the exercises and the free time activities have contributed to this wholeness of the character. And now the actor can be confident that he can put this character in any place, with any group of people, under any circumstances, and the Mask will react organically, true to his or her own nature.

Tying up Loose Ends for the Character

The actor must now prepare the last stage of development for the character. After the weeks spent developing the Mask and extending his behavior into innumerable circumstances, the actor will feel the need to make an appropriate final statement for the character. The last assignment is designed to help the actor seek the words and the situation that will best express what other facets of the character's personality he wishes to reveal. Further, with the last showing before the group, the actor will be given the opportunity to take the character away with him at the conclusion of the course.

Tying up Loose Ends for the Character
"I think his need for protection and friendship is something that should be brought out in my final piece—the intense need for help, comfort and protection."

Step 50: Finding the Right Words

TIME

As many class sessions as are needed to see all the exercises individually. After class commentary and further rehearsal in free time is utilized. The exercises are then repeated for one more session.

PURPOSE

To use words and ideas written by others to express the character's thoughts—to make a bridge between the character and the written script; to explore other sources of thought besides dramatic literature; to explore and develop a situation that reveals a final statement about the character; to continue the search for economical, interesting form by shaping the piece to communicate clearly to an audience.

HOMEWORK

From published material in any form other than dramatic literature (poetry, essays, biography, letters, fiction, nonfiction, etc.), put together a monologue which your character will speak in a five-to-seven-minute situation that has a beginning, a middle, and end. *The monologue must seem as if it is the character's own words and thoughts.* You may change the pronouns and proper names in the material to those appropriate to your character's world. You may use several works to piece together one monologue. Bring appropriate clothing and use objects to create the environment and situation. You may talk to imagined characters, use characters from this group, or you may choose to be alone, speaking aloud to yourself. Your reason for speaking must be specific and motivated. This is the final assignment and you will want to use it as an opportunity to find the right words to develop one last facet of the character's personality or life-style.

PROCESS

After the first showing in class and subsequent discussion, the exercises will be rerun a second time *without the masks*. The rerun without the masks provides a new experience for the actor as he prepares to leave the work. Its purpose is to make the adjustment needed to take the character away while leaving the mask in the classroom. The actor must trust that the character can exist without the mask.

OBSERVATIONS

It would be helpful to make the homeowrk assignment for this exercise long in advance of the anticipated work session in class. The actor will need to sift through much written material before finding the right words for his Mask. The assignment is gratifying because it culminates the work process of the entire sixteen weeks. It provides a final statement for the character in a form that is clean and clear. The actor must move outside his own imagination in order to find the words for the character. He must examine a great deal of material before he can find what is right and true for the character's personality and circumstance. Nondramatic literature is used because it forces the actor to probe writers and styles that he may not usually examine. Some examples of final exercises from past classes:

1. A black preacher's son, who had defied his father's teachings and had rebelliously cut himself off from society, finally confronted all the Masks and revealed his inner torment and asked for understanding and help. The actor's material was from Ralph Ellison, James Baldwin, and other black authors.

2. A sex-starved spinster was secretly a "peeping Tom," using binoculars and a telescope to invade her neighbors' privacy. While watching a couple make love, she took notes on what they were doing and put them in her diary for "future reference." The actor used sex manuals and cheap, erotic novels as sources for her words.

3. A goofy, uninhibited character who had no place to live except a box in a wide, open field, set up a special romantic dinner party, complete with candle and flower. He invited one of the other Masks and then proceeded to ask for her hand in marriage. The actor used love poems and song lyrics for his material.

FINAL NOTE

As a result of this exercise, then, the character's action has become a union of three inspirations: the actor, the mask, and the writer. The relationship that has now been formed is not unlike that which the actor uses in rehearsal for a play; the actor's imagination (the creation of the role) must depend upon the writer's imagination (the play and the character as written). This will be discussed more completely, along with suggestions on how to use mask characterization techniques while working on a role, in part 2, the section "Bridging the Gap to the Role."

Part 2: The Actor's Guide

The Actor's Guide

"The thing I learned most from the class was that there's a part of every personality in me, and they're all available to me. I've become stronger—I'm a much fuller person."

Questions for Steps 1–50

This section is designed to guide the actor in answering questions that will help him create the mask characterization. They are by no means the only questions the actor should answer for himself. They are merely set down as a springboard for his own written exploration. The questions should be answered honestly and specifically. If a question triggers a discovery, an emotion, a problem, or a solution, the actor should immediately express that discovery before going on to the next question. The importance of this journal cannot be stressed enough. For the actor to learn to respond organically and then define for himself what has happened is a necessary tool in his craft. As you recall from part 1, the exercise steps are as follows:

Step 1: First Encounter
Steps 2–3: Choosing the Mask
Step 4: Exploring the Room
Step 5: Looking at Yourself and Others
Step 6: Picking Apples
Step 7: Sitting on a Chair
Step 8: Jumping on a Trampoline
Step 9: Pulling a Rope
Step 10: Digging Stones and Feathers with a Shovel
Step 11: Pumping Water from a Well
Step 12: Sitting and Reading in a Chair
Step 13: Hanging Pictures on a Wall
Step 14: Setting the Table with Company Coming
Step 15: Crawling in a Tunnel
Step 16: Flying a Kite
Step 17: Rowing a Boat
Steps 18–20: Re-creating the Centers of Crawling in a Tunnel, Flying a
   Kite, and Rowing a Boat
Step 21: Using a Score
Step 22: Using a Score with Specific Inner-Sensory Condition and/or an
   Environmental Condition
Steps 23–25: Using a Score with a Specific Location
Step 26: Doing a Private Task
Steps 27–29: Doing a Private Task with Specific Circumstances
Step 30: Making Your Body Speak
Step 31: Doing a Simple Action

Step 32: Doing a Simple Action with an Obstacle
Step 33: Doing a Simple Action with an Absurd Obstacle
Step 34: Waiting for a Bus
Step 35: Riding a Subway Train
Step 36: Attending a Reception Honoring the President of the United States
Step 37: Trying on Clothes
Step 38: Exploring Language
Step 39: Finding Yourself in a Place with Someone
Step 40: Receiving a Surprise Call
Step 41: Calling to Get a Job
Step 42: Getting Interviewed
Step 43: Keeping Busy at Home Alone
Step 44: Keeping a Conflict Hidden
Step 45: Speaking about Personal Matters on the Telephone
Step 46: Going to a Party
Step 47: Getting Stuck
Step 48: Getting into Trouble
Step 49: Going on an Outing
Step 50: Finding the Right Words

Step 1

This is your first encounter with the mask. You have seen only one mask; however, all the masks are as varied and contradictory as the one you viewed today. The following questions will help you articulate the impressions and images that you experienced. Take your time, and remember, this journal is for yourself and for the character whom you will create. Be as clear and honest as you possibly can in your answers.

1. What was your first impression when you saw the mask on the model?

2. Were you attracted to the mask? If not, why?

3. Did your attitude change the more times you spent with the mask? How?

4. What was it like when the masked model touched you? Made eye contact with you?

5. Did you make initial contact with the mask? How did it feel?

6. What images came to mind when the masked model walked? Ran? Skipped? Sat down? Crawled? Lay down?

7. What did the model's face look like when the mask was removed? Had she become part of the mask for you?

8. What are your feelings about wearing this type of mask? How do you feel about the fact that you and the mask will be together for sixteen weeks? Are you frightened? Challenged? Excited?

Step 2

As you begin your mask exploration keep your journal and this page of the guide in easy access to you. The following questions will guide you in your exploration. However, always go beyond them. Make your own statements. Allow whatever thoughts are forming to be written in your journal. Don't think! Just write! These thoughts are part of the formation of your character. Do not neglect them.

1. What was your immediate reaction to each mask as you put it on? Did the reactions change as you stayed with the mask for a while?

2. Did the silence in the room affect you? How?

3. Did you feel the atmosphere was private enough to permit yourself to freely explore your feelings through your body?

4. Do you enjoy the feeling of having your face covered? Does it change the way you behave?

5. Are you physically and imaginatively open to each mask? If not, what is holding you back? Try to locate your inhibitions and name them.

6. Do you feel alone in the room? If not, how are other people affecting your work? How can you shut them out of your consciousness? (Ask yourself these questions often to see if your reaction to people around you changes as the work progresses.)

Step 3

You will be selecting the mask you will work with for the period of time you are taking this course. The following questions are guidelines for your impressions in the final selection and commitment to the mask.

1. Which masks particularly interest you? Scare you? Excite you? Challenge you?

2. Which masks seem to reflect your personality? In what way?

3. Which masks seem opposite to how you behave and feel most of the time? In what ways?

4. Which masks bring out something in you which you usually do not express? What are those qualities?

5. Which masks can you "live" with for an extended period of time? Why?

AFTER THE MASK IS CHOSEN

1. How did you feel when you were asked to line up and choose the masks? Tense? Worried? Excited?

2. How does your mask fit? Can you wear it comfortably for a long period of time? Does it need adjustment?

3. What is it like to have this mask for yourself?

4. What do you expect to find out about this mask?

5. What do you expect to find out about yourself?

6. What do you want to accomplish for yourself in this class?

Step 4

This is your first experience with dealing with your mask and your work space for a long period of time. Answer the following questions regarding this experience and add your own further comments.

1. What were your feelings during free time? Were you comfortable? Uncomfortable?

2. When you began to explore the room, what did you notice. Be specific. Angles of room? Color? Size? What about the mirrors? The ceiling? The floor? The objects? The room?

3. Do space and objects seem different behind the mask?

4. Do the space and objects seem familiar? Unfamiliar? Comfortable? Uncomfortable?

5. What happened when you touched objects with your hands? Feet? Head? Back? Stomach? Other parts of the body?

6. When you changed your personal tempo in approaching the object, did you feel differently toward it?

7. What was it like when you hopped? Jumped? Ran? Skipped? Rolled? Crawled?

8. What was it like when you changed direction? When you walked sideways? When you walked backward?

9. What did you notice when you listened to objects? When you rubbed them? Hit them? Scratched them? Tapped them?

10. What interested you in the objects? Pick three and discuss your interest.

11. What is it like to work for yourself and not be concerned with performing?

Step 5

You have now spent a session inspecting yourself and others. These questions are designed to guide your thought process as you record in your journal.

1. What did you see when you looked at yourself in the mirror? Was it different when you moved? Sat down? Tilted your head? Moved your arms around?

2. What did you see when you looked at yourself through the mask (i.e., you, the masked person, looking at your hands, your feet, your stomach, your chest)?

3. When you looked at other masked persons, what did you feel? What did you see? Were they different from you? How? Were they similar? How?

4. Did you feel comfortable looking at other individuals? Did you feel uncomfortable?

5. What did you feel when other masked persons looked at you?

6. Did you find it difficult to explore without being able to deal with a social persona? In what ways?

Steps 6—10

These exercises were designed to exercise sensory images that motivate behavior. After each exercise, answer and expand on the following questions:

1. How free are you?
2. Can you stretch more even if you are now at your maximum?
3. What parts of your body are still closed to you?
4. How far are the images carrying you?
5. What kind of images do you respond to best?
6. What makes you lose concentration?
7. How are you getting in your own way?

Steps 11–14

In these exercises, you were creating a place and a specific task. The exercise always began with a basic reality and then was extended to a greater extreme. These questions will guide you in the discoveries made.
1. How specific is your imagery?
2. Can you minimize your movements more but continue to sustain the energy to accomplish the task?
3. Are you looking at tasks, people, yourself, differently?
4. Do you have a specific tap on cataloging your physical behavior?
5. What parts of you are you still not using?
6. Have you stretched your powers of belief?

Steps 15–17

These exercises are known as The Big Three. They are more intense than previous exercises. Each exercise is divided into three parts. The questions are grouped for this division.

PART I

1. Were you able to create the environment? What was most clear for you? What was unclear?
2. Doing an inventory of the five senses (touch, taste, smell, sound, sight), which of these sensorial re-creations was easiest? What was most difficult?
3. What happened to your body when the circumstances changed? Re-create in your mind the journey taken and write down what took place for your body, your mind, your emotions, and your other responses. Did your behavior change? How?
4. What was it like to use sound?
5. What are you feeling right at this moment?

PART II

1. How did you feel when the center took over?
2. Have you ever experienced the change in your body form by trig
gering imaginative circumstances?
3. What was most pleasurable about discovering the center? What was
most difficult?
4. When you shook out and started over, how easy was it to re-create
the center?

PART III

1. What was it like to use this center in trying to catch a bus?
2. What was it like to use this center when lying down? Walking in and
out of the doors? Taking a chair and moving it? Sitting down in the chair?
Looking at other people? Making physical contact with another mask?
3. Did your breathing change with the new center?
4. How did your tempos, rhythms, emotions, change with the new
center?
5. Were there any responses with this center that you have never experienced before? What kind? Was it comfortable? Uncomfortable?

Steps 18–20

These exercises allowed you to recall and re-create centers previously
discovered.

1. What was it like to recall and re-create the last burst of energy experienced in the exercise? Did you find it easier than you had anticipated?
Did you find it more difficult? Were the emotions different from the first
experience in the tunnel? The clouds? The boat?
2. When the center was re-created, did you feel as if another person
was growing out from inside you? How different was that person from
you? Was the person different when you looked in the mirror? When you
sat down in the chair?
3. What were the differences when you threw off one center and re-
created another? Did your emotions change? Did you attitude change toward those around you?
4. Was there one particular center which was easier than the others?
One which was more difficult?

Steps 21–22

New centers have been discovered in these exercises. You are beginning to see the limitless resources you have in creating movements, emotions, and responses that are not part of your everyday persona. Continue to examine this discovery.

1. What's it like to create physical and sensorial circumstances in creating the center? Are you finding that it is easier? In what ways? In what ways are you having difficulty?

2. When you breathed in the number, what happened to your body? Your emotions? Your responses to the room? People? The instructor?

3. What was it like this time to try to catch the bus and then to miss it?

4. Is your sound changing? How? If not, what is it doing?

5. What sensation did you have when you communicated the sound to the instructor?

6. What do you feel about the instructor? Do you feel differently toward the instructor when you have different centers? Do you feel differently toward others in the class?

7. Describe the physical center that propelled you into the instructed activities and the accompanying organization of the body? How did you feel and think about yourself operating from the center?

8. What changes occurred when you chose a specific inner sensory condition and/or an environmental condition?

9. Did you make your choice difficult enough? If not, why? If so, how?

10. What was it like to go through the score of actions without the instructor guiding you?

11. Are you anticipating centering the energy? If so, what ways can you prevent yourself from doing it?

Steps 23–25

You should ask yourself these questions after each new center is discovered in an exercise:

1. How quickly can you create the circumstances and move to the crisis moment? In what ways is it easy?

2. How much do you anticipate now? Is this less of a problem? What do you think is happening?

3. How clear are the images? How fast are they coming?

4. Is your imagination easier to tap? When tapped, how fast does the imaginative circumstance flow into your body?

5. Do you feel the sense that there are other behaviors and emotions yet untapped in you? If you located another center of energy, do you feel you will expose another part of you? Can you identify any behaviors/ emotions yet untapped? If so, how can you get to them?

Steps 26–29

You have now experienced finding new centers based upon physical tasks and imagery placement.

1. What were the circumstances?

2. How did it feel to have someone watching you?

3. Who was watching you?

4. Where did you hide the tool you were carrying?

5. How did it feel when it was first placed inside you?

6. Where was your center?

7. How did the center affect your physical behavior, running, sitting, leaning, greeting, etc.?

8. How did it affect your breathing?

9. How did it affect your thinking?

10. What kinds of behavior have you not experienced yet? What task and tool might provide you with new centers and experiences? What will you choose next?

11. Are there any *constants* in your feelings or behavior from exercise to exercise?

Step 30

You are exploring language with your whole body.

1. Was it fun for you to take a word or phrase through your body?

2. Did you permit yourself to go with your first impulse and later economize upon and refine that body statement?

3. Did you like watching others? Did their statements inspire you? Intimidate you?

4. Are you expressing what you are feeling at any given moment through your body or are you still keeping your thoughts covered and private?

Steps 31–33

Making your objectives clear, simple, and effective, in spite of the obstacle, is very important in all of your work. It is particularly necessary when you are speaking with your body and not with your mouth.

1. What were your choices? Were your situations too complicated?
2. Were you able to communicate simply and truthfully?
3. What could you have done to make your statements more clear?
4. Is your imagery alive and affecting you?
5. Can you operate logically even if the circumstances and obstacles are illogical?
6. Do you like "talking" with your body instead of verbalizing your thoughts?

Steps 34–36

You are now in the process of exploring how your behavior is affected by other people—how relationships cause you to react.

With each of these exercises write down the specific circumstances, what your reactions were, and what was fully realized.

1. Is your Mask beginning to respond in ways that you would not do? In what ways?
2. How does your mask character walk? How does he react to the specific situations placed in?
3. When your mask character is under pressure, what happens?
4. When your mask character is in an absurd situation, what happens?
5. When your mask character relates to people, what are his feelings? Responses? Is he secure? Insecure? Aggressive? Passive?
6. How are you feeling right at this moment?
7. What were your choices for the improvisation?
8. Where was your center?
9. How were you affected by the waiting? By the worsening conditions?
10. How are you affected by other people?

Steps 37—38

More and more stimuli are now reaching you. Examine carefully and objectively how they are affecting your behavior.
1. How are you feeling now about working alone? How do you feel when you make contact with others?
2. What kinds of clothes are you finding attractive? Unattractive?
3. How does your mask character's tastes measure up to yours? Better? Worse? The same?
4. What was it like to explore language with your new clothes?
5. What was it like to relate to other people with words now that you have your new clothes?
6. What is it like to incorporate words into your free time?
7. What is free time like for you now?
8. Are there any *constants*, consistent behavioral patterns, which keep recurring in spite of changes of clothing and new relationships.

Step 39

You have begun to test yourself in specific environments and with new relationships.
1. What were the circumstances of each improvisation?
2. Did the relationship bring out something new in you?
3. How did the other person affect you? Be specific in recounting what you felt.
4. How did the environment affect you?
5. What was it like to communicate nonverbally? Did you find the right moment for the one word or phrase?
6. Did you and your partner sense a natural ending to the improvisation?
7. Did you have difficulty redoing the improvisation? Was it truthful the second time? Was the form clearer, more succinct? Did you learn something new about yourself the second time?

Steps 40–41

Who you are (the Mask) is starting to emerge. You have learned some facts about the character's past and present life from the phone calls and you have begun to test how the character reacts under pressure from people on the other end of the phone.

1. For each phone call, write down the specifics: Whom did you talk to? What was the content of each of the conversations?

2. What did you find out about the character's behavior? How does the character react under pressure? How were you most comfortably seated in the chair? Most uncomfortably seated?

3. Where were you and how did each place affect you?

4. Was your subtext different from what you were saying? What were you doing with your hands? Your feet? Your whole body while you were talking?

5. What was it like to be able to speak? Did you feel free? Inhibited? Did you permit your thoughts and verbalizations to go through your whole body?

Step 42

Now the character truly exists. How does it feel?

Write down your immediate response to the interview. How much like the mask character are you? How unlike are you? Are you surprised at the creation? What were all the facts you learned about the character's life?

Now, after you have written in the first person, write your experience as your mask character. Once you have written this, note the difference between you and your mask character.

1. How did it feel to be in front of all those people? Frightened? Excited?

2. When did you relax?

3. What was happening to your body during the interview? Your hands? Your feet?

4. Did you lie to the people?

5. What impression do you think you made on people?

The character is formed. However, your search for deepening the Mask's personality and discovering the consequent behavior is just beginning. You must ask yourself at the end of each day's session the following questions:

1. What is left?
2. What don't you know?
3. What situations can you set up that will tell you more?
4. Who can you tap that you haven't yet worked with?
5. What objectives can you give yourself that will put the character under greater stress or give him more pleasure? What tasks or activities will help you?
6. What was the character like at age eighteen? Twenty? Thirty? What will he be like?
7. What would happen if . . . (and you create the circumstance)?

Each time you complete an exercise, write down your response to the exercise as the character. Then write down your response to your character as the actor. Begin to separate the two, so that you may see what you have created from yourself.

Step 43

Discovering how the character behaves in his/her own territory is very important. Answer these questions for the character.
1. Where were you? What did it look like? Did you feel totally private in your space?
2. What colors and textures surrounding you particularly pleased you? What objects pleased you?
3. How did you occupy yourself? What amused you? What did you dislike?
4. What was it like to be alone at home? Were you lonely? Did you like it better than being with people?
5. What did you discover about the way you handle yourself and objects in private? Do you want other people to see you do these things? How is your private behavior different from how you act in public?
6. For the actor—did the character choose different tasks and react to objects differently than you had anticipated?

Steps 44—50

All of these exercises are designed to help you extend the boundaries of your character's life and personality. The form that you choose to communicate the character's ideas and behavior must be simple, clear, and truthful. For each of these final exercises, write down the circumstances and what you learned about the character.

In addition to the discoveries you make about the character in these exercises, record any class comments that are helpful about the work. Be objective and honest with yourself about your communication skills. Are you specific? Are you able to make people understand your objectives? Your subtext? Can you find a situation or a task which would better serve your ideas? Is the form you chose simple and economical? What can you do to clean it up further?

Some individual questions for the specific exercises:

STEP 44: KEEPING A CONFLICT HIDDEN

1. Did your situation change drastically when you went to nonverbal behavior? Were you able to solve the problem?

STEP 46: GOING TO A PARTY

1. Did the character behave as you expected?
2. How did other partygoers affect your spirits?

STEP 49: GOING ON AN OUTING

1. Were you frightened at the thought of taking the character out of doors and away from the protective atmosphere of your classroom?
2. Did you feel daring among strangers?
3. Do you feel greater satisfaction knowing that you can go anywhere, talk to anyone, and feel completely real and organic as the character at all times?

STEP 50: FINDING THE RIGHT WORDS

1. How did you feel when you had to remove your mask?
2. Do you feel you could become this character, without the mask, at any time now?
3. Do you feel you can create another character as deep in personality, as complete in past history, as full throughout your whole body, voice, and imagination?

Bridging the Gap to the Role

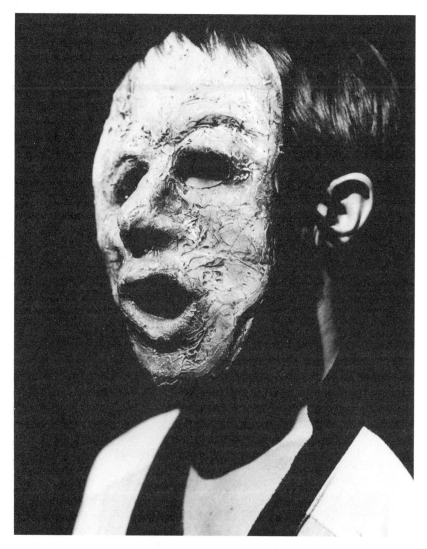

Bridging the Gap to the Role
"The mask—does it inspire us to a character or simply allow us to be a character?"

This final section is addressed directly to the actor in order to help him identify how to proceed from this point. After going through the arduous classwork, the actor will need to examine and assess for himself just what has been experienced and accomplished. He knows he has created a complete character, but he probably will not know precisely how this happened, or how he has changed inwardly or outwardly. Further, he will want to know how to use what he has learned when he moves out of the classroom and into the rehearsal space.

Talking to the Actor

It is sixteen weeks, or ninety-six hours later. You have left the mask in the classroom, thrown the character's clothes in the laundry basket for a much needed cleaning, put away or given away the once precious objects that belonged to the world of the character. Now what? To examine mask characterization and extract from the process techniques for building a character in a play, it will be helpful to look at what has happened to you as a result of this work.

Looking at the Actor

Mask characterization has given you a much broader and much deeper awareness and insight into your physical self and your emotional, imaginative self. You work with responsibility and discipline in order to call upon that creative self. Your body works better for you. You have greater physical strength. You have exercised daily and released tension areas. You have stretched both your body and your *concept* of what it can do for you. You have allowed your body to "talk" to you. You trust it more. After all, your physical behavior has consistently given you clues to what you have been feeling and thinking, why shouldn't you have more confidence in how it can feed your inspiration? The change of center and accompanying organization of your body parts have made you move, breathe, think, and speak in new ways.

You are more willing to risk experience with your body. You are less likely to sit and think out a solution; you want to move in order to find out how you feel. You are not afraid to let things happen to you. Not only is physical improvisation easier and more fun than it was before, but it is also a useful tool for exploring an event or an idea. You will not put boundaries or limits on your physical behavior before the discovery occurs. You will stay open and try anything now.

You operate physically with more economy and simplicity You know when you are using too much of you to communicate an idea. You can pare down an expression of the idea and use three gestures instead of six. You are aware of when a physical gesture is specific and complete. You can find other parts of your body to help you express the gesture. Your idea of physical logic has been expanded to allow more interesting behavioral choices.

The same kind of opening, stretching, and risk-taking that you have accomplished for your physical instrument have been strengthening in your emotional instrument as well. You have increased your sensory awareness. You can look at people, objects, and environments and actually feel them through your whole body. You are less likely to dismiss things. You enjoy the sensations more tangibly now that they reach inside you.

Your creative impulses and instincts have been uncovered. You have touched upon your personal feelings and have *unmasked* them and used them to inform your objectives. Your ability to concentrate has increased enormously. You can give yourself to the moment, keeping your attention riveted to what is happening. You are not anticipating or stepping outside of yourself. You are *there*, unafraid of the experience, in tune with what you are feeling and thinking. However, you are able to separate yourself from the character, and you can clearly analyze your behavior and articulate your feelings and discoveries.

You have exercised and utilized aspects of your personality and colors of your emotions that you do not usually permit to surface when building a scripted character. You have not just thought about these hidden facets of yourself, you have *used* them to create the Mask. You are completely cognizant of when you are behaving truthfully and fully. With the mask on, each one of your thoughts, feelings, and actions organically follows the one prior to it.

You exercise greater discipline over yourself. You carry an exploration out to the maximum degree, even if you are tired, bored, or frightened. You have more control over the use of your body and imagination. You can tap your inner resources to inform your outer behavior.

Take a look at yourself in the mirror. Do you look any different? Possibly you are a little less tense and a little thinner. However, it is probable that all of the benefits of the mask-work are not immediately visible. It is far more important for you to realize that these things have *all happened to you* in the course of the work. You only need to *recognize the depth and breadth of the change to allow it to function for you in the rest of your work*. It will be equally as valuable to examine the character you created to determine how the mask-work will profit your craft.

Looking at the Character

In all probability, the character that you have created from the mask is the fullest, most complete that you have ever realized. You may have begun the work process thinking that you would create someone totally different from you, that the character would come from your preliminary judgments about the mask. Instead, you found that parts of your own personality and experience were magnified and absorbed to create the personality of the Mask. A side of you blossomed and came forward to a greater extent than other sides of you. You moved past your ideas about characterization, past the cliches and stereotypes, and developed the Mask from your less accessible emotions and ideas. The character *came* from you, yet it was *not you*.

The sequential development of the Mask was similar to the development of a role for you. You knew little about the character at first, but after trying many things, a pattern of behavior formed and you understood what you were doing and why. This character's body is probably more alive and vital, his behavior more completely formed and controlled, than your past creations.

This character is a real person, fully rounded, with a past history that informs all the "present" ages you have explored. You understand the character's problems, and you have experienced most of the climactic moments in his life. You also understand how this person functions normally without conflict or crisis. You know about the little touches and colors that make up his individual personality. This creation is a product of your instrument: your body, your voice, and your imagination. And it is such an interesting person! These are some of the newly found and better-developed resources that you bring to your craft of acting. Now you can examine how best to use the mask techniques for building a characterization in a play.

Looking at the Script

The play is a creation of a world with all or most of the circumstances defined by the playwright. Each character has a function to serve in relation to the play's central ideas and themes. The character's basic psychology and behavioral patterns are stipulated by the playwright within the dramatic action.

Excellent textbooks and teachers abound who can explain in detail how to build a role based on the evidence that has been analyzed. This book is not addressing itself to that work, nor is it suggesting that mask characterization invalidates or even substitutes for play and character analysis. The program which you have been through is supplementary to the investigation of the text. It focuses on you and your creative powers. It suggests a way to help you tap and use your resources to fill the stipulations of the playwright's character.

It has already been suggested that the mask is somewhat akin to the character in a play. It is a sophisticated creation, carefully and artfully designed. The painting and sculpting of the face present some "given circumstances" for the character, though of course, these are highly flexible and subject to personal interpretation. The mask, like the script, exists before the actor tackles the filling in and fleshing out of the role.

If you have taken a careful assessment of your accomplishments with the mask characterization process, you know that you have developed a highly accessible and receptive instrument to bring to the text. When working on a script, it should take you much less time to open yourself to your personal feelings. The role is as much of a safety and a cover as the mask. You can use it to uncover the parts of you that are demanded by the play.

Working with the Script

It would be valuable to locate a physical and/or emotional center for the character and then realign your body to operate around that center. Moving about and working with the center will help you clarify the thoughts and actions of the character. You may need to try numerous centers before one feels right and true.

It will be easier to refrain from playing stereotypes or caricatures because in the mask-work you have experienced the delicious taste of creating a real person who copes with life out of necessary drives and protective defenses. To this end, fill in a total life history for the character, not only to understand his past but to get a clear knowledge of his inevitable future after the curtain has come down. You will want to know how the character lives normally when he is not involved in the action of the play. This is not just a question of defining a past history; this is filling in the character's personal tastes and habits.

You will not only need to think out the character's life-style completely but will need to experience as much of it as you can yourself. Naturally, you will be doing this at every rehearsal with the rest of the cast. However, this process has taught you that more time and experience are necessary to a full development of the character. It will be helpful to improvise daily, probably at home, to find out what gets your character in trouble, how other people affect him, what are his secret hopes and dreams. On the most ordinary level, you will want to experience how he sets the table, makes the bed, prepares a personal toilette, dresses, runs for a bus (remember that?), etc.

It is necessary to have a very clear understanding of the character's thinking at every moment in the play. When you have accomplished this, you may want to find a way to communicate the thinking nonverbally. This will prevent you from heavily relying on your eyes or your face to express your ideas. When you take the thought through your whole body and speak with other parts of you, you will find other, more interesting means of communicating the ideas.

Give yourself permission to experiment earlier than usual in rehearsal. Remember, *the role is your mask*, and you do not have to protect your social image and limit your explorations, you will not waste precious rehearsal time dabbling about, afraid to make physical or mental commitments to the objectives. You will let go sooner and find out more. After experiencing the totality of the creation of a mask character, you will always know when the character from the script is layered and filled on the inside and formed economically and clearly on the outside. You must now allow yourself to be somebody else, from top to toe!

Afterword

As you by now have discovered, the process of creation is a mysterious one. Does the mask *inspire you* or does it *allow you* to create the character? How does it happen? When did it happen? Every individual who has undergone this process might have different answers to those questions. It would certainly be helpful to reread your journal, now that you are finished, and see if you can find personal keys to when, where, and how the creation came about. However, the more important result of this investigation is that the masks have kept you aware of the *other person* you were creating. You were always *using you*, but you were *developing someone else.*

Both the instructor and the actor will surely feel encouraged by the results of the mask characterization process. The instructor has seen the actor working optimally, with vitality, economy, and enthusiasm. The actor has been excited with his desire to perform and would like to try again to create more characters of equal width and breadth. The next time through the process, the Discovery period can be shortened because the actor's instrument will be more accessible and prepared to explore, develop, and extend the intuitions and impulses. Several Masks could be created within the same time framework.

In addition, the mask characterization process not only offers the actor useful techniques to improve his craft but also provides enormous possibilities for personal growth. If the actor has successfully uncovered and utilized his richest creative imagination to form the character, then his own sense of competence, assertiveness, autonomy, and confidence will have been exercised and enhanced. The desire for totality and excellence will be the goal for future projects and relationships.

Sample Class Schedule

Week	Day One	Day Two	Day Three
1	First encounter with one mask	Choosing the mask	Final choosing of the mask
2	Steps 4, 5	Step 5 (repeat); Steps 6, 7	Steps 8, 9, 10
3	Step 8 (repeat); Steps 11, 12	Steps 13, 14	Step 15
4	Repeat walks from Steps 15, 16	Repeat walks from Steps 15 and 16; Step 17	Repeat walks from Steps 15, 16, 17; Step 21 (repeat three times)
5	Steps 22–25; Step 26	Steps 27–29; repeat using a score or private task	Repeat using a score or private task; Step 30
6	Steps 31–33	Extend free time; Step 34	Steps 35, 36
7	Step 37	Repeat Step 37; Step 38	Repeat Step 38; Step 39 (twice)
8	Repeat Step 39 three or four times	Free day	Steps 40, 42
9	Step 41; Continue Step 42	Continue Step 42	Continue Step 42
10	Step 43	Step 44	Rerun nonverbal version of Step 44
11	Step 45	Step 45	Step 45
12	Rerun of Step 45	Step 46	Step 47
13	Free day	Step 48	Step 48 continued
14	Step 48 continued	Repeat of Step 48	Step 49
15	Free day	Step 50	Step 50 continued
16	Step 50 continued	Step 50 (without masks)	Final discussion

Index of Exercise Steps